OECD Reviews on Local Job Creation

City of Talent Montreal

AN ACTION PLAN FOR BOOSTING
EMPLOYMENT, INNOVATION AND SKILLS

This work is published on the responsibility of the Secretary-General of the OECD. The opinions expressed and arguments employed herein do not necessarily reflect the official views of the Organisation or of the governments of its member countries.

This document and any map included herein are without prejudice to the status of or sovereignty over any territory, to the delimitation of international frontiers and boundaries and to the name of any territory, city or area.

Please cite this publication as:
OECD (2017), *City of Talent Montreal: An Action Plan for Boosting Employment, Innovation and Skills*, OECD Publishing, Paris.
http://dx.doi.org/10.1787/9789264268661-en

ISBN 978-92-64-26865-4 (print)
ISBN 978-92-64-26866-1 (PDF)
ISBN 978-92-64-26867-8 (epub)

Series: OECD Reviews on Local Job Creation
ISSN 2311-2328 (print)
ISSN 2311-2336 (online)

Photo credits: © iStockphoto.com/mustafahacalaki.

Corrigenda to OECD publications may be found on line at: *www.oecd.org/publishing/corrigenda*.
© OECD 2017

You can copy, download or print OECD content for your own use, and you can include excerpts from OECD publications, databases and multimedia products in your own documents, presentations, blogs, websites and teaching materials, provided that suitable acknowledgement of OECD as source and copyright owner is given. All requests for public or commercial use and translation rights should be submitted to *rights@oecd.org*. Requests for permission to photocopy portions of this material for public or commercial use shall be addressed directly to the Copyright Clearance Center (CCC) at *info@copyright.com* or the Centre français d'exploitation du droit de copie (CFC) at *contact@cfcopies.com*.

Preface

Throughout OECD countries, cities and metropolitan regions are at the forefront of efforts to increase prosperity and create more and better jobs. City leaders and officials can play a crucial role to address the pressing issues of rising inequalities, poor labour market integration of some disadvantaged groups, and sluggish productivity growth, which disproportionately affect urban areas. They are often best placed to design and implement integrated, tailored and effective local strategies thanks to their local knowledge and their ability to mobilise resources within their jurisdiction and beyond.

However, municipalities are not always responsible for all of the policy spheres that can impact the performance of their cities. It is often the case that multiple tiers of government are responsible for the management of labour market, skills development, innovation and entrepreneurship programmes. While increased legislative and fiscal autonomy at the level of cities can contribute to the achievement of their full potential, institutional reforms alone will not guarantee that public policies will yield better outcomes. Other success factors include better collaboration between all partners involved as well as governance mechanisms that encourage stakeholder engagement and buy-in.

This report aims to provide the municipality of Montreal and its partners with evidence-based recommendations to improve the economic and social performance of the city, and Quebec and Canada more generally. It proposes a strategy to create more and better jobs in more productive firms that make full use of the talent available, thus providing incentives for young people to gain more skills and to engage in innovative activities. This necessitates targeted policy interventions in all policy areas to boost SME development, stimulate innovation within firms of all sizes, and encourage the development and full use of skills, especially among the immigrant population. Ambitious strategic objectives pursued by all local stakeholders within an integrated governance framework are needed to set Montreal on a path towards to a high skills and high productivity equilibrium.

I hope that the municipality of Montreal and its partners will find the research and guidance presented in this publication both informative and actionable. A more inclusive growth is within reach if all stakeholders in Montreal come together to pursue a new ambitious strategy.

Lamia Kamal-Chaoui,
Director, Centre for Entrepreneurship, SMEs,
Local Development and Tourism, OECD

Foreword

This publication was prepared by the Local Economic and Employment Development (LEED) Programme of the Organisation for Economic Co-operation and Development (OECD), under the leadership of Sylvain Giguère. It is part of the LEED Programme's series of OECD Reviews on Local Job Creation which deliver evidence-based and practical recommendations to policy makers on how to better support employment and economic development at the local level.

The authors are Sylvain Giguère and Pierre Georgin, of the OECD, and Normand Roy, consultant. The authors would like to acknowledge the valuable contributions of Jonathan Barr, Nathalie Cliquot and Michela Meghnagi, of the OECD. François Iglesias should also be thanked for his assistance with the preparation of this report.

The authors would also like to thank the departments, municipal and metropolitan representatives, as well as organisations from the private and non-governmental sectors who participated in the project interviews and roundtables, and provided data, documentation and comments critical to the production of the report.

Table of contents

Acronyms and abbreviations 7

Executive summary 9

Chapter 1. A new strategy is required to address Montreal's challenges 11
    Recent governance changes in Montreal 13
    Opportunities and challenges associated with the move towards metropolis status .. 15
    Note 17
    References 17

Chapter 2. Employment and the local economy in Montreal, an international comparison 19
    Balancing skills supply and demand to stimulate the creation of quality jobs 20
    How Montreal compares 21
    Complementing the diagnosis 22
    Some conclusions on the strengths and weaknesses of Montreal's economy 36
    Notes 37
    References 37

Chapter 3. Initiatives in Montreal: Key findings 39
    Theme 1: Improved co-ordination between employment, skills development and economic development policies, and how they are relevant to Montreal 42
    Theme 2: Creation of a productive local economy – adding value through skills and avoiding the low skills equilibrium trap 54
    Theme 3. Supporting entrepreneurship, innovation and economic development ... 55
    Theme 4. Ensuring that growth is inclusive – economic development and skills development to promote the integration of all individuals into the labour market 69
    Note 73
    References 73

Chapter 4. An action plan for Montreal 75
    Strand 1. Structure, reinforce and more effectively target support for SMEs 78
    Strand 2. Encourage bottom-up and cross-cutting innovation processes 79
    Strand 3. Stimulate demand for skills through training and research 80
    Strand 4. Raise the level of skills of the workforce 82
    Strand 5. Facilitate the integration of immigrants into the labour market and leverage their potential for boosting innovation 82
    Implications for governance and metropolitan status 84
    References 86

Tables

2.1. Selected OECD metropolitan areas 25
2.2. Changes in sectoral shares in GDP, Montreal............................ 29
2.3. Comparative assessment of the Montreal metropolitan area.............. 37

Figures

2.1. Balance between skills supply and demand, administrative regions of Quebec, 2011... 22
2.2. Balance between skills supply and demand, selected metropolitan regions of North America, 2011 23
2.3. Population annual average growth rate, 2000-14......................... 24
2.4. Old-age dependency ratio 2014 25
2.5. Net international and interprovincial migration, Montreal CMA, 2002-14 25
2.6. Educational attainment of the population aged 25-64, 2011.............. 26
2.7. GDP per capita (USD 2010), 2012 27
2.8. GDP per capita (USD 2010), 2000-13..................................... 28
2.9. Labour productivity (thousand USD 2010), 2012 28
2.10. Employment by sector of activity, Montreal, 2014....................... 29
2.11. PCT patent applications per 10 000 inhabitants, 2008 31
2.12. Innovation by Canadian SMEs in the past three years (percentage of SMEs surveyed), 2014.. 32
2.13. Participation rate, 2014 34
2.14. Comparison of unemployment rates for immigrant and Canadian-born populations, 2014.. 34
2.15. Share of unemployed people in the labour force, 2013 35
2.16. Share of unemployed people in the labour force, selected North American cities, 2000-14.. 35
3.1. The public policy framework: results from the dashboard 41
3.2. Flexibility, co-ordination and local data............................... 42
3.3. Creation of a productive economy through skills........................ 50
3.4. Entrepreneurship, economic development and innovation 55
3.5. Inclusive growth... 69

Follow OECD Publications on:

 http://twitter.com/OECD_Pubs

 http://www.facebook.com/OECDPublications

 http://www.linkedin.com/groups/OECD-Publications-4645871

 http://www.youtube.com/oecdilibrary

http://www.oecd.org/oecddirect/

Acronyms and abbreviations

ACS	Attestation of college studies
AMT	Metropolitan Transport Agency
BAS	Business assistance service
BDC	Business Development Bank of Canada
BINAM	Montreal Newcomers' Integration Office
BTMM	Board of Trade of Metropolitan Montreal
CAMAQ	Quebec Sectoral Aerospace Workforce Committee
CCTT	College Centre for Technology Transfer
CED	Canada Economic Development for Quebec Regions
CEGEP	General and vocational college
CEM	Metropolitan Employment Council
CFDC	Community Futures Development Corporation
CJFA	Canada Job Fund Agreement
CLD	Local development centre
CLE	Local employment centre
CMA	Census metropolitan area
CPMT	Commission of Labour Market Partners
CRE	Regional Conference of Elected Representatives
CRPMT	Regional Council of Labour Market Partners
CS	School board
ETS	*École de Technologie Supérieure*, engineering faculty, University of Quebec
ICT	Information and communication technology
ISQ	Quebec Institute of Statistics
LMDA	Labour Market Development Agreement
LMI	Labour market information
MAMOT	Ministry of Municipal Affairs and Land Occupancy
MEESR	Ministry of Education, Higher Education and Research
MEIE	Ministry of the Economy, Innovation and Exports
MESI	Ministry of the Economy, Science and Innovation (formerly MEIE)
MI	*Montréal International*
MICC	Ministry of Immigration and Cultural Communities
MIDI	Ministry of Immigration, Diversity and Inclusion
MMC	Montreal Metropolitan Community
MTESS	Ministry of Labour, Employment and Social Solidarity
NEET	Not in Education, Employment or Training
OECD	Organisation for Economic Co-operation and Development
QI	*Quartier de l'Innovation*
RCM	Regional county municipality

ACRONYMS AND ABBREVIATIONS

SMEs	Small and medium-sized enterprises
StatCan	Statistics Canada
STC	Skills training certificate

Executive summary

Montreal is the driving force of the Quebec economy and possesses a wealth of assets that could transform the city into an innovative and economically dynamic metropolis on the world stage. Montreal's workforce is growing as a result of international immigration, while the presence of high-quality tertiary and research institutions both attracts and produces world class talent. The economic structure of Montreal features both highly structured industrial clusters and a fertile ecosystem of entrepreneurs and SMEs, which nurtures the development of innovative enterprises in high value-added sectors. Other assets of Montreal include a high quality of life and an environment that encourages innovative activities.

Despite these positive attributes, Montreal has not yet been able to translate these assets into improved job creation and higher standards of living for the general population. Although the Canadian economy performed better than the OECD average in the years following the economic crisis of 2008, the economy of Montreal remained relatively stagnant. The labour force features both a large number of overqualified workers and a low level of productivity per worker. Similarly, structurally high levels of unemployment are reinforced by the poor integration of newcomers into the labour market, particularly immigrants and those with fewer qualifications. These conditions indicate a labour market landscape that is not conducive for the creation of more and better quality jobs.

There are a number of factors that explain Montreal's labour market paradox. Despite the city's education and training infrastructure, the level of educational attainment amongst Montreal's population is relatively low, which limits the pool of skills available to the local economy. Montreal also features a high concentration of very small enterprises with product market strategies that are solely oriented towards the local market, presenting few incentives to invest in skills, innovate or move up the value chain into higher value-added production. In comparison with other North American cities, the economy of Montreal falls into a low skills and low productivity trap. As a result, the local labour market of Montreal has grown increasingly polarised between high-quality jobs in high value-added sectors and low-skilled jobs that require few or no qualifications in sectors like retail, healthcare and social assistance. There is a risk that this will entrench inequalities and widen gaps, leaving behind a significant proportion of the labour market in low-quality, poorly paid jobs that offer limited career progression opportunities.

Faced with these challenges, public authorities, economic actors and civil society organisations have implemented various initiatives to promote the acquisition of skills, stimulate the development of productive and innovative activities and boost the employability of certain target groups. However, the impact of these efforts is stunted by a lack of responsiveness, resources, and co-ordination between initiatives in the portfolios of employment, economic development, education and training, and immigration. The public authorities also need to adjust their interventions to a new reality of innovation and local development that is driven by networks and collaboration between various actors, and no longer follows traditional sectoral barriers or linear value chains.

New policies are needed to push Montreal onto a trajectory towards a high skills and high productivity equilibrium. Improving Montreal's ability to generate more and better jobs means making better use of available skills, as this is the key to enhancing innovation and productivity while encouraging the local population to acquire new skills. Montreal needs to break the self-fulfilling vicious cycle of poor qualifications and low-skilled jobs, broaden the horizons of young people and small enterprises, and embrace the potential created by immigration.

These objectives can only be achieved by adopting a global, integrated strategy that is championed by Montreal's diverse network of local actors. With strong leadership, the municipality of Montreal can promote the emergence and effective implementation of such a strategy by mobilising local stakeholders and rolling out an ambitious programme to transform public action. The evolving governance of Montreal presents an opportunity to promote the establishment of an integrated and stakeholder-led policy framework. This strategy could be translated into a series of specific, co-ordinated actions in the areas of economic development, innovation, vocational education and training, employment and immigration.

Proposed action plan

1. Structure, reinforce and more effectively target support for SMEs
- Promote SMEs internationalisation
- Stimulate innovation within SMEs

2. Encourage bottom-up and cross-cutting innovation processes
- Continue to support collaborative initiatives that mobilise all stakeholders
- Broaden innovation processes by encouraging user-based and incremental innovation within firms
- De-compartmentalise industrial clusters

3. Stimulate demand for skills through training and research
- Strengthen links between educational institutions and firms, especially SMEs, to promote skills utilisation through applied research
- Encourage universities to actively align with and engage in local economic development priorities
- Facilitate employer engagement in the design of vocational education and training curricula

4. Raise the level of skills of the workforce
- Smooth educational pathways through partnerships between universities and community colleges (CEGEPS)
- Make vocational education and training more flexible

5. Facilitate the integration of immigrants into the labour market and leverage their potential for boosting innovation
- Ensure that Montreal's skills needs are taken into account when determining provincial intakes of skilled immigrants
- Better tailor training offers to the needs of immigrants
- Ensure that the process of streamlining support services for immigrants priorities labour market integration and attachment
- Facilitate enterprise creation by immigrants
- Put in place tailored support for youth of immigrant origin

Chapter 1

A new strategy is required to address Montreal's challenges

Montreal is a vast metropolitan region which, in 2014, had a population of just over 4 million. The city possesses a wealth of assets that could transform it into an innovative and economically dynamic metropolis both in North America and within the OECD. These include a huge potential reservoir of talent, whether among the local populace, educated in Montreal's top quality further education institutions, or among the many qualified immigrants who are attracted to the city each year. This is a crucial source of development in the current economic climate characterised by the growing importance given to innovative activities, both technological and non-technological, which demand a high level of skills. The relative dynamism of Montreal's population, due largely to international immigration, means that employers can rely on an abundant workforce. The economic fabric of Montreal is diversified, as evidenced by the presence of both highly structured industrial clusters in high added value sectors and a fertile ecosystem of entrepreneurs and SMEs in emerging sectors such as health, information and communication technologies, including video games, but also in the social and collaborative economy.

Like many other large urban regions of the OECD, Montreal is undergoing major changes on the demographic, spatial, economic and social fronts associated with the phenomenon of metropolisation: urban sprawl, greater mobility, increased nuisance levels (pollution, congestion) and also social and spatial segregation and fragmentation. The Quebec metropolis is also facing serious challenges in terms of employment, skills and economic development. It has high levels of structural unemployment compared to other North American metropolitan regions. The local labour market tends to be polarised between quality jobs in cutting-edge sectors and lower quality jobs requiring few qualifications, meaning that a significant share of the labour force is over-qualified. Integrating young people and immigrants into the labour market and retaining talented individuals are also serious challenges. According to some studies, Montreal's economic fabric, which is composed principally of SMEs and micro-enterprises, appears to be characterised by low productivity and insufficient dynamism, thus limiting the productive capacity of the local economy.

In the face of these many challenges, public actors need to implement co-ordinated, integrated and sufficiently flexible strategies to adjust to local situations. National policies or local initiatives in a particular field risk being ineffective when adopted in isolation and without taking the specific characteristics of Montreal's economy into account. For example, increasing the educational attainment of the local population will certainly not lead to satisfactory results in terms of quality job creation unless the local labour market offers opportunities to workers which reflect their skills level and unless employers make full use of the skills of their workforce.

The municipality of Montreal and the Quebec Government are currently holding discussions aimed at giving Montreal a new status. This is an opportunity for establishing an overall strategy, mobilising all players and co-ordinating their actions, whilst giving them sufficient margin for manoeuvre in order to adjust programmes and initiatives to the specific needs of Montreal's economy. Efforts to improve metropolitan governance must continue with a view to enhancing the potential for quality job creation in Montreal and putting the city on a trajectory towards reaching a high skills and high productivity equilibrium.

Recent governance changes in Montreal

The complexity of governance in Montreal has for a long time damaged the coherence of public action and its clarity for socio-economic actors. In its Territorial Review published in 2004, the OECD highlighted the damaging effects of institutional isolation and fragmentation in decision-making, at the level of both the "agglomeration" and the metropolitan region of Montreal (OECD, 2004). Efforts to consolidate metropolitan governance undertaken since then have certainly made strides towards greater rationalisation of institutional structures. In terms of economic development, there has been a clarification of the respective roles of the Quebec Government and of the municipality of Montreal, with the latter having taken the upper hand in this field by creating PME MTL (a network of experts supporting entrepreneurs and businesses) following a re-organisation of the network of local development centres (CLDs). Yet despite these recent reforms, the institutional and financial resources to be allocated to the municipality of Montreal for implementing an integrated economic and skills development strategy are still a burning issue.

Montreal is currently divided into 19 different boroughs, each with a mayor, municipal councillors, budgets and their own resources. A reform implemented at the beginning of the new millennium merged the entire island into a single city whilst nonetheless giving the boroughs a broad margin for manoeuvre. The basic idea which led to the merger was that certain responsibilities naturally spilled over the territorial limits in existence prior to the merger and that the fiscal burden should therefore be shared equitably among the beneficiary population. However, a referendum process carried out in 2004 led to municipal "de-mergers" and the re-creation of 15 municipalities on the island of Montreal in 2006. Although the Island of Montreal therefore has 16 municipalities, the city of Montreal is by far the largest in terms of population with 1 744 323 inhabitants in 2014, because it contains 88% of the population of the Montreal Agglomeration (1 988 243 inhabitants in 2014). The latter is the administrative and political body which manages shared services, including the police, fire fighters and public transport, and has an assessment role. Despite the de-mergers, the principle of joint responsibilities and fiscal equalisation has survived under the new structure. An Agglomeration Council, headed by the Mayor of Montreal and comprising a majority of Montreal City Council members, is the agglomeration's political body.

The Montreal Metropolitan Community (MMC), a political and administrative body created in 2001, manages various services across the census metropolitan area (CMA)[1] of Montreal. Although the MMC includes 82 municipalities, the city of Montreal accounts for 43% of its population, and it is the Mayor of Montreal who chairs the Metropolitan Council.

The annual budget of the municipality of Montreal was USD 4 882.5 million in 2015. Of that amount, 21.5% was earmarked for public security, 16.6% for debt servicing, 10.4% for leisure and 10% for public transport. General administration accounts for 9.1% of spending and corporation taxes for 9.0%. Administration costs and the effectiveness and quality of the services provided for citizens represent major challenges for the city. The municipal administration is therefore working towards a harmonisation of the services offered by the 19 boroughs and, in the summer of 2015, it created an organisational performance service responsible for tackling the issue of service quality and efficiency. In terms of income, over two-thirds comes from the land tax, and this proportion rises to three-quarters if we include the share of services paid for by the reconstituted cities, which are themselves largely dependent on income from the land tax.

The municipality of Montreal bears additional costs deriving from its status as principal city of the census metropolitan area and Quebec metropolis. These costs, for which there is no relatively accurate estimate, relate to intensive use of the Montreal infrastructure by non-residents, school transport provided by the Montreal transport company (STM), specialist police services and the concentration of immigrants in the Montreal region. Some of these costs have been recognised in the context of past reforms, such as the reforms which led to the creation of the MMC and the Agglomeration Council, and in specific, limited-duration fiscal agreements between the Quebec Government and the municipal authorities, notably in the Agreement to recognise the special status of Montreal of June 2008.

There are other factors which tend to affect the finances of the municipality of Montreal, such as the characteristics of the population in terms of poverty levels and unemployment, which are structurally higher than in suburban areas and the rest of Quebec. Moreover, several government services provided by the Quebec Government, such as the employment and economic development services, involve lower per capita expenditure in Montreal than in the rest of Quebec, due to a sharing formula which takes on board major fixed costs, irrespective of the population concerned.

The MMC has a modest budget of CAD 115 million per annum, because its main sphere of activity concerns planning, principally in relation to land use, the environment, transport and the economic development of the metropolitan region. That revenue comes essentially from the shares paid to it by its 82 constituent municipalities. The provincial government also finances specific projects on an *ad hoc* basis.

Box 1 gives an overview of the current responsibilities of the various layers of government or administration active in the Montreal region. The fact that a number of responsibilities are shared means that a high degree of consultation and collaboration is require in order to take coherent decisions and measures which offer openings for mutual enhancement in the pursuit of common objectives in Montreal.

Box 1. **Distribution of competencies in Canada, Quebec and Montreal**

Since Canada is a federal country, this means that certain constitutional responsibilities lie within the exclusive remit of the federal government, such as national defence, foreign affairs, currency, interprovincial commerce including interprovincial transport and communications, citizenship, criminal law and employment insurance. The provinces have jurisdiction over municipal affairs, natural resources, civil law, education, social affairs and health. In several areas, such as economic development, employment, the environment, agriculture and culture, to name but a few, responsibility is shared, as appropriate. Furthermore, the federal government may intervene in provincial matters by way of programmes with shared costs or programmes which it alone finances in certain cases, but it must obtain the consent of the provinces.

The municipality of Montreal has competencies principally in the fields of public security, grant-aided housing renovation programmes, the environment, town planning and the triennial capital assets programme. In addition, the municipal council is called upon to frame, harmonise or approve certain decisions taken by the borough councils.

> Box 1. **Distribution of competencies in Canada, Quebec and Montreal** (cont.)
>
> The borough councils shoulder certain responsibilities in terms of urban planning, removal of residual material, culture, leisure, social and community development, management of highways and parks, green spaces, human resources, fire prevention, non-fiscal charging and financial management.
>
> The main responsibilities of the Agglomeration Council of the Island of Montreal, an entity which covers the municipality of Montreal and the municipalities in the agglomeration, lie in the areas of property value assessment, security services, the municipal court, social housing, aid for the homeless, the waste management plan, water supply and wastewater treatment, public passenger transport, street and highway management, economic development, including for tourism purposes, beyond the boundaries of a member municipality, nature parks, and also the planning and development plan for the agglomeration.
>
> The Montreal Metropolitan Community (MMC) is a planning, co-ordination and financing body operating across the range of its competencies which include land use, economic development, artistic and cultural development, social housing, equipment, infrastructure, services and activities of a metropolitan nature, public transport and the metropolitan arterial system, planning of wastewater management, clean air, air remediation and sewerage. The MMC has particular responsibility for preparing the Metropolitan Land Use and Development Plan (MLUDP), which aims to provide an integrated and coherent vision of land use and development for the metropolitan area, and the Metropolitan Economic Development Plan (MEDP).
>
> *Source:* Ville de Montréal (2015) and the Canadian Parliament.

Opportunities and challenges associated with the move towards metropolis status

Montreal is in discussion with the provincial government about obtaining a new status. Although discussions are still in progress and the details of a possible agreement are not yet known, the guiding principles and broad outlines are fairly well delineated between the parties. First, under the Canadian Constitution and in accordance with the practice in force in Quebec since the early days of the Canadian Confederation in 1867, the cities are the "creatures" of the provincial government, which means that they have only delegated, subordinate powers and that they are required in numerous cases to obtain authorisations on a case-by-case basis from the provincial authorities before being able to amend existing regulations, or before enacting new regulations, or even before undertaking any initiative in a field where they have no explicit, *a priori* authority to act. Moreover, they possess only delegated, limited powers in terms of taxation and financing. Montreal is therefore aiming to obtain a status as a "government of proximity", which would entail greater regulatory, financial and fiscal flexibility and also certain responsibilities in relation to economic development and support for enterprises, for example. This increased flexibility is felt to be necessary in order fully to meet the challenges facing the metropolis, especially regarding social issues (vagrancy management, the fight against poverty, immigrant reception, social housing management), economic issues (support for economic development and the process of innovation; international relations and promotion) and employment (integration of immigrants into the labour market, for example). Suitable financial tools, such as perennial overall budgets dedicated to municipal action areas and coupled with rigorous accounting procedures, will need to accompany these increased responsibilities. The allocation of new sources of autonomous revenue, in addition to the property tax, would also make it possible to harness some of the wealth created as a result of the economic development effort put in by the municipality of Montreal. Here again, tools to monitor expenditure, including operating costs, plus rigorous accounting procedures would form part of a new enabling law whose main aim would be to substitute transparency and *a posteriori* accounting for the current *a priori* authorisations which mean that the municipality of Montreal has to turn to the Quebec Government even in trivial cases such as speed limits on municipal roads or shop opening hours.

This institutional reform would have several advantages. First, it would increase Montreal's autonomy in terms of adopting regulations for the promotion of economic, environmental and social well-being, for example as regards renovating abandoned buildings or vacant plots of land whose expropriation could be facilitated. It would permit the delegation of powers and service responsibilities in areas where the principle of subsidiarity should logically apply, such as housing. Finally, it would open up the possibility of providing more active support for economic actors, especially SMEs starting up in innovative and emerging sectors. Being granted greater responsibilities and resources means that the municipality could also allow various under-utilised or vacant municipal buildings to be converted. In terms of employment, promotion of skills and economic development, the change in the status of the municipality of Montreal and the negotiations between the various layers of government with regard to transferring competencies provide an opportunity to define more clearly the role of each stakeholder. Greater flexibility could be given to those local actors involved in responding to specific territorial problems and a higher level of integration between strategies could be achieved. The municipality of Montreal must seize this opportunity to develop its sphere of action and the way in which it supports local economic development.

In view of the metropolitan scope of certain challenges, the competencies of the MMC will certainly need to be reinforced. At the same time, given the concentration of population, activities and wealth on the Island of Montreal, it seems essential for the municipality and the Agglomeration Council of Montreal to continue to play a central role in the future system of metropolitan governance. The purpose of this report is not to suggest precisely what division of competencies between administrations would be best for Montreal; rather, its aim is to contribute to the broad discussion regarding the means of obtaining the most satisfactory results in terms of creating quality employment, productivity, innovation and the integration of disadvantaged groups into the labour market. In view of the discussions under way between the Quebec Government and the municipality of Montreal, the territorial layers of the municipality and the agglomeration will feature prominently in this report.

The second chapter of the report will show how Montreal performs in terms of economy growth, skills, innovation and employment in comparison with national and international peers. It will attempt to pinpoint the strengths and weaknesses of the local economy using key economic and labour market indicators and criteria established by the OECD. The third chapter will provide an overview of the measures and initiatives taken in the various areas covered by this review. It will highlight the challenges that still have to be addressed and suggest potential areas for improvments in light of international experience. Finally, this report will suggest courses of action on the basis of these findings.

Note

1. The territory of the MMC, a political and administrative entity, differs slightly from that of the CMA, which corresponds to an economic and social area defined by Statistics Canada according to a measurement of the number of movements of people for work or other purposes.

References

OECD (2004), *OECD Territorial Reviews: Montreal, Canada 2004*, OECD Publications, Paris, *http://dx.doi.org/10.1787/9789264105980-en*.

Ville de Montréal (2015), *2015 Budget*.

Chapter 2

Employment and the local economy in Montreal, an international comparison

This chapter assesses the strengths and weaknesses of the Montreal metropolitan area in terms of an adequate balance between the skills of its people and its production capacity. Key socio-economic data for Quebec's largest city provide a picture of how Montreal performs compared to 18 selected cities in other OECD countries.

Balancing skills supply and demand to stimulate the creation of quality jobs

Skills are crucial, not only to people's employability and their chances of career advancement but also to business productivity and innovation. Economic theory categorises skills and knowledge as key drivers of economic growth. In today's competitive economic climate where innovative activities, both technological and non-technological, are increasingly important, regions with a highly educated population unquestionably have the edge. But investing in education and training is not enough on its own to guarantee job creation and better productivity. Account must also be taken of the scale of demand and the use of skills by local employers. For a variety of reasons, businesses may fail to make the best possible use of the skills available (Froy, F., S. Giguère and M. Meghnagi, 2012). When employers do not demand a high level of skills, and individuals' skills are not used to the full, productivity may be weakened as a result. The quality of local jobs may suffer in terms of pay, job security and promotion prospects. In that case, increased investment in skills development may not bring the anticipated results.

Conversely, regions may have a high level of activity in research and development, investment and entrepreneurship, indicative of a high demand for skills. But if skills supply is poor, this can translate into lost opportunities for economic development and job creation. A region's prosperity will thus depend largely on the ability of local stakeholders to ensure a proper balance between supply and demand for high-level skills.

In connection with this study, the OECD LEED Programme developed a statistical diagnostic tool to help measure, for the Montreal region, the extent to which the population's skills adequately match the needs of local production activities. This is done by comparing a skills supply index, representing the local population's ability to contribute to high-value-producing activities, against a skills demand index, which identifies the importance of this type of activity in the local economy. These indices are calculated in relation to the other regions against which the city of Montreal is compared. Box 2 describes the methodology used.

> ### Box 2. **The diagnostic tool**
>
> The OECD LEED Programme has developed a statistical diagnostic tool to help assess the balance between skills supply and skills demand. The level of skills supply is estimated as the percentage of the population with post-secondary qualification. Skills demand is calculated using a composite index based on the percentage of the population in medium- and high-skilled occupations and gross value-added (GVA) per worker. The indices are standardised using the interdecile method and compared against the median for the regions included in the comparative analysis.
>
> Depending on the relative level of skills supply and demand, local economies can broadly fall into four different categories: those experiencing a low-skills equilibrium (where skills supply and demand are both relatively low); those experiencing skills gaps and shortages (where skills supply is relatively low but demand is relatively high); those experiencing a

> **Box 2. The diagnostic tool** *(cont.)*
>
> skills surplus (where skills supply is high and demand low); and those experiencing a high-skills equilibrium (where both supply and demand are relatively high).
>
>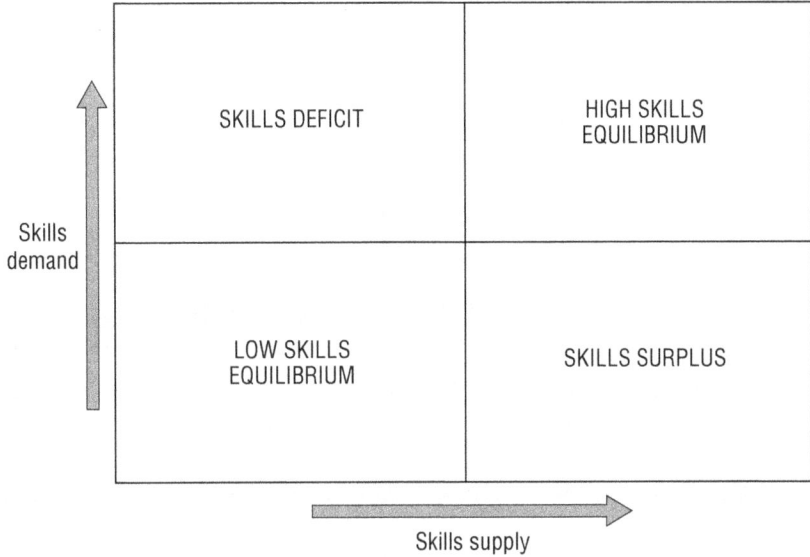
>
> The methodology is explained in greater detail in F. Froy, S. Giguère and M. Meghnagi (2012), "Skills for Competitiveness: A Synthesis Report", *OECD Local Economic and Employment Development (LEED) Working Papers*, 2012/09, OECD Publishing.

How Montreal compares

Similar ecosystems are often found in OECD metropolitan areas in terms of skills and innovation. These urban territories typically have a large proportion of highly skilled people, high productivity and numerous cross-links between a range of economic actors who make up formal and informal networks. Increasingly, concentrations of highly skilled individuals are found in the main urban centres in many countries, such as the USA (Berry and Glaeser, 2005; Bacolod et al., 2009) or the United Kingdom (Tochtermann and Clayton, 2011). This may be because employment opportunities there are more numerous and varied, and wages and salaries are higher, so that individuals' skills can be exploited to better effect (OECD, 2014a). Densely populated regions also make for easier movement of knowledge and ideas, whether deliberate or involuntary, which adds to the formation of human resources and stimulates the creation of activities that are innovative and bring sizeable value added. This does not, however, rule out the possibility of high unemployment. OECD work has identified an "urban paradox", in that many large cities in the OECD countries also have pockets of poverty, high unemployment and a large proportion of low-paid jobs requiring few skills (OECD, 2006; OECD and China Development Research Foundation, 2010).

The position of Montreal relative other administrative regions of Quebec (Figure 2.1) is somewhat unusual in comparison with other countries. Montreal is certainly the region best served in terms of skills supply, measured as the percentage of the population holding a post-secondary diploma. The Laval administrative region, part of the Montreal Metropolitan

Figure 2.1. **Balance between skills supply and demand, administrative regions of Quebec, 2011**

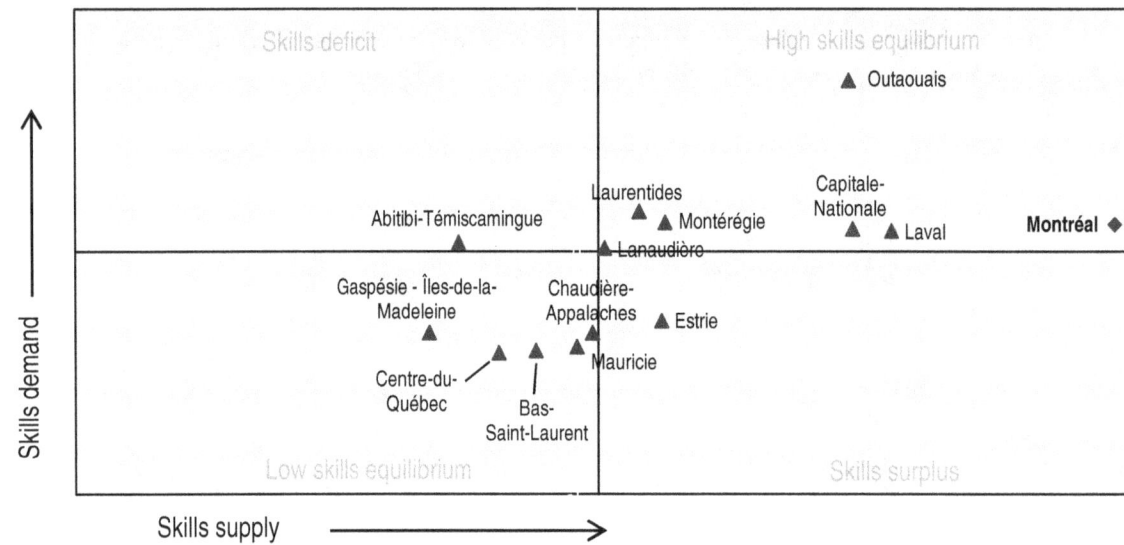

Source: OECD (2014b), *Employment and Skills Strategies in Canada*, OECD Publishing, Paris, http://dx.doi.org/10.1787/9789264209374-en.

Community, is also well placed in this regard. But the level of skills demand, measured in terms of skilled jobs and productivity, is far lower in Montreal and Laval than in the Outaouais (a reflection of the benefits enjoyed by the economy of the federal capital) and similar to that seen in the administrative regions of the Laurentides, Montérégie and the National Capital Region. Whilst the labour markets of some of these regions are heavily dependent on the Montreal economy, this situation is markedly different from that in most OECD countries where there tends to be a clear divide between the main urban centres and the other regions of the country in terms both of skills supply and skills demand, for the reasons stated previously.

Given the similarities alluded to between the large cities in OECD countries, Montreal can also be compared with other metropolitan areas in North America. The Canadian cities of Toronto and Vancouver were selected along with all US cities having a population of between 3.5 and 10 million. Thus the indices for skills supply and demand were calculated in relation to the other metropolitan areas. Figure 2.2 sets out the diagnostic tool's findings. According to this comparison, Montreal's level of skills demand is relatively low in comparison with the rest of selected cities. The other two large Canadian cities also show relatively poor scores in this domain. For skills supply, Montreal also scores relatively poorly compared with the other Canadian cities, but slightly better than Dallas, Miami, Phoenix, Detroit and Houston.

Measured against comparable North American cities, the Montreal economy thus show weaknesses both in the level of demand for skills, suggestive of a lack of dynamism in production capacity and productivity, and in the level of skills supply. Relative to these cities, Montreal falls into a low skills equilibrium.

Complementing the diagnosis

This diagnosis can be fine-tuned using an analysis of the local data that are directly or indirectly relevant to skills supply and demand, enabling a clearer picture to be drawn of the strengths and weaknesses of the Montreal local economy in an international context. The rest of this chapter places the socio-economic position of the city of Montreal in

Figure 2.2. **Balance between skills supply and demand, selected metropolitan regions of North America, 2011**

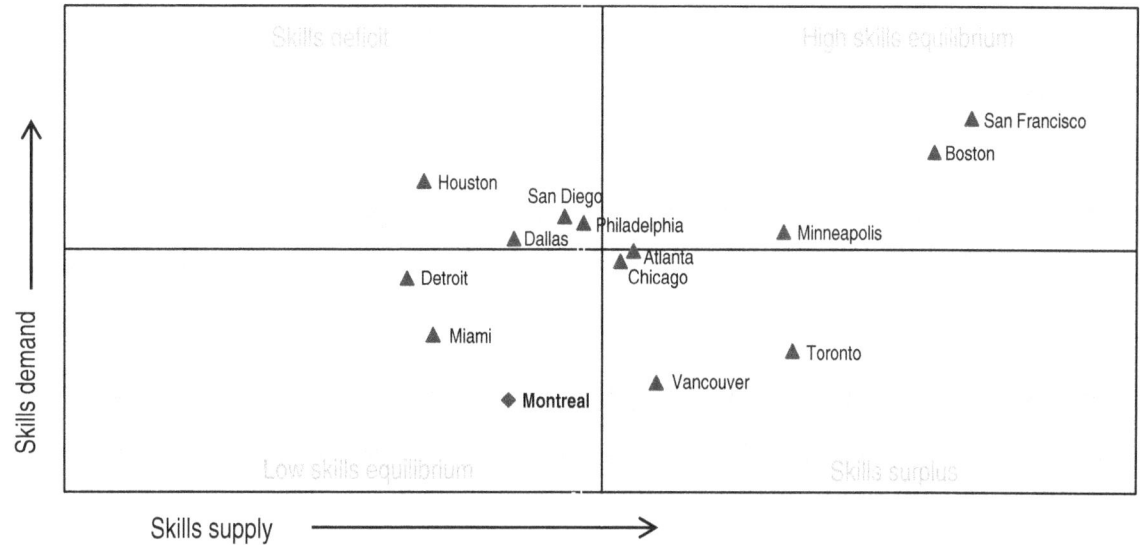

Source: LEED Programme calculations based on data from national statistical institutes and the OECD.

perspective by comparing it with 18 cities in OECD countries (see Table 2.1). These cities are similar to Montreal in size, their ranking in national urban hierarchies or their sectoral specialisation. The comparisons between countries and between North American cities were made using available OECD data for metropolitan areas. Where data allowing comparison at this level of aggregation were not available, the analysis was performed at the level of the census metropolitan areas (CMAs) for the main Canadian cities, using data from Statistics Canada. Additional data from the Quebec Institute of Statistics (ISQ) were also used.

Table 2.1. **Selected OECD metropolitan areas**

Barcelona (ES)	Frankfurt (DE)	Melbourne (AU)	Toronto (CA)
Boston (US)	Hamburg (DE)	Milan (IT)	Toulouse (FR)
Busan (KR)	Lyon (FR)	Prague (CZ)	Vancouver (CA)
Chicago (US)	Manchester (GB)	San Francisco (US)	
Dublin (IE)	Marseille (FR)	Stockholm (SU)	

Availability of labour and skills in Montreal

An analysis of the demographic growth in Montreal provides an indication of the pool of labour, skills and talents potentially available in the city.

With a population of 4.4 million in 2014, the metropolitan area of Montreal, as defined by the OECD, is home to 53.5% of the population of Quebec and is the second largest conurbation in Canada after Toronto (6.9 million). Between 2000 and 2014, Montreal's population grew by an average of 1.3% a year. Whilst this rate is lower than in Toronto and Vancouver, the demographic of Montreal can be seen as relatively dynamic compared with other OECD metropolitan areas (Figure 2.3).

During this period, Montreal's population as a proportion of the total population of Canada rose only slightly (from 12% to 12.4%), but as a proportion of the total for Quebec, it rose from 49.9% to 53.5%.

2. EMPLOYMENT AND THE LOCAL ECONOMY IN MONTREAL, AN INTERNATIONAL COMPARISON

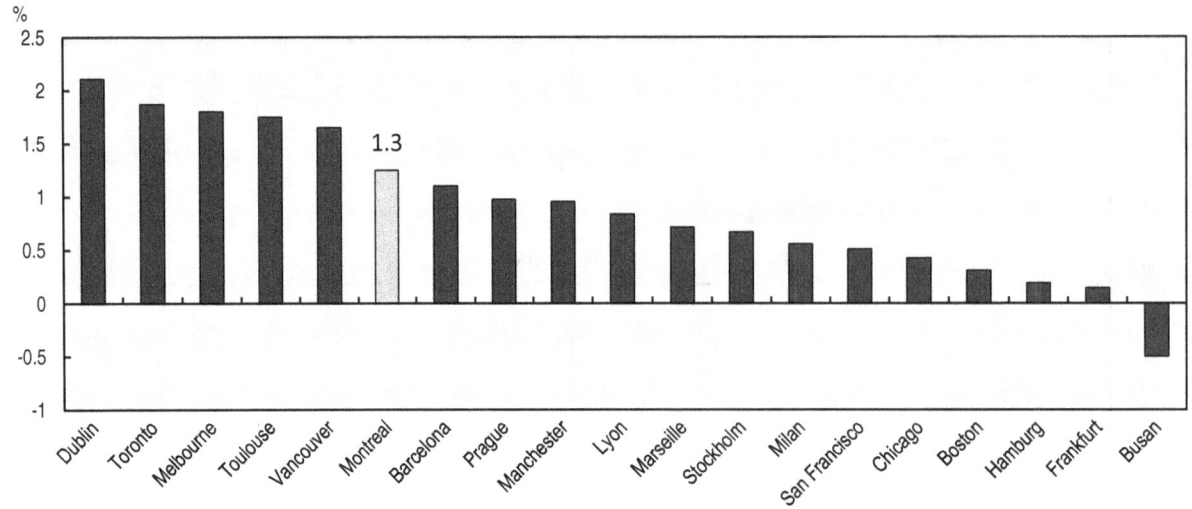

Figure 2.3. **Population annual average growth rate, 2000-14**

Source: OECD (2016), "Metropolitan areas", OECD Regional Statistics (database), http://dx.doi.org/10.1787/data-00531-en.

The rapid expansion of the periphery and the phenomenon of urban sprawl meant that the proportion of the total population of the metropolitan area living in the city core – the Island of Montreal – decreased (from 51% in 2006 to 49% in 2011), whilst population density increased from 337 inhabitants per km^2 in 2000 to 400 in 2014. This phenomenon, known as "suburbanisation", can be observed in all the large Canadian cities (Gordon and Janzen, 2013) and in a number of OECD countries too. More specifically, between 2001 and 2011, the gap between population growth inside and outside city cores was particularly wide in Mexico, Korea, Spain, Greece and the USA (Veneri, 2015).

During the period 2000-2014, average annual growth in the population aged 65+ (up 2%) was greater than that of the working age population (age 15-64) (up 1.5%), which meant that the demographic dependency ratio between these two population groups increased from 18.9% to 20.3%. The "greying" of Montreal's population remains relatively limited, however, compared with that of other OECD metropolitan areas (Figure 2.4). The figures for Italian and German cities, in particular, are far higher than those for Montreal, and over the past 10 years, these cities have seen a major decline in their working-age population, creating a major challenge for employment policy, pension schemes and social security systems.

As in other OECD countries, the relative demographic dynamism of Montreal is largely due to international immigration. Thus, the number of non-immigrants living in Montreal fell by 20 520 between 2006 and 2011 whilst the immigrant population grew by 52 560 over the same period (MMC, 2013). Counting for the Montreal Census Metropolitan Area, the number of new immigrants resident for less than 10 years was close to 320 000 in 2012. Whilst net international migration has been broadly positive over the past 15 years, Montreal has tended to lose population to other regions in Quebec and the rest of Canada (net interprovincial migration was down 9 996 in 2014) (Figure 2.5).

In 2012, almost 75% of new immigrants to Montreal were economic migrants, that is to say they were accepted on the basis of their social and occupational profile, their skills and their ability to contribute to the economy (MMC, 2013). The average educational level of this group is well above that of non-immigrants: the proportion of individuals qualified to

Figure 2.4. **Old-age dependency ratio 2014**

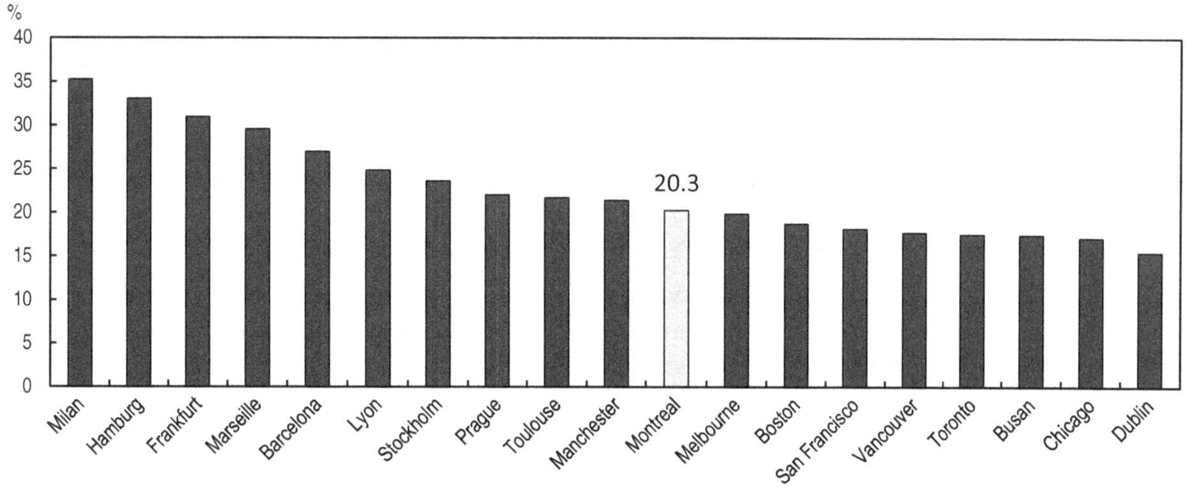

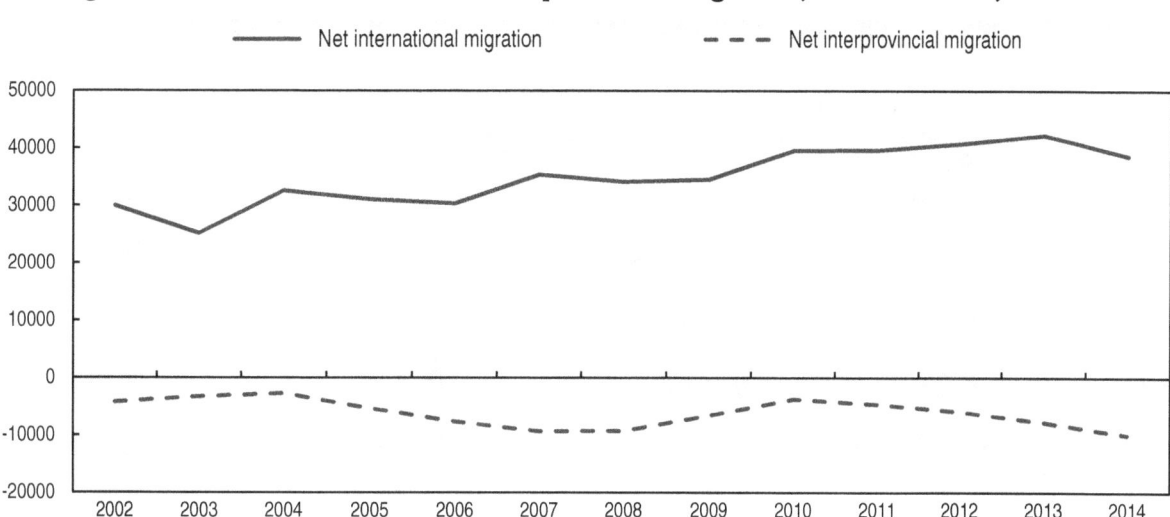

Source: OECD (2014b), *Employment and Skills Strategies in Canada*, OECD Publishing, Paris, http://dx.doi.org/10.1787/9789264209374-en.

Figure 2.5. **Net international and interprovincial migration, Montreal CMA, 2002-14**

Source: Quebec Institute of Statistics (ISQ).

degree level (*baccalauréat* in Quebec) or higher is 49% for immigrants aged 25 and over arriving after 2001, as against 23.8% for non-immigrants.

The percentage of persons born abroad as a proportion of the total population is higher for Montreal (22.6%) than for Canada as a whole (20.6%), but it is relatively small compared with Toronto (46%) and Vancouver (40%). The Island of Montreal has the most international immigrants, and the majority of new immigrants to the metropolitan area are found here (Statistics Canada, 2013).

The various population categories moving to the Montreal metropolitan area include a large number of international post-secondary students (CEGEPs and universities): 27 934 in 2013, which is 49% up on the figure for 2006 (MI and CEM, 2015). Whilst this trend is also seen in Toronto and Vancouver, Montreal has stayed ahead of the other large Canadian cities in this respect in recent years. Montreal is also, after Toronto, the Canadian city which takes in the most specialised temporary workers (13 905 in 2013, an increase of 96% over 2006). According to the MI and CEM study (2015), retaining these skilled population groups is a major challenge for the Montreal metropolitan area at a time when the population is ageing and there is a growing need for a skilled workforce in certain sectors such as aerospace, ICT and the life sciences. The three main obstacles identified by this study were access to employment, a limited knowledge of French and an insufficient understanding of the immigration process. Similar problems are often identified in the European context where the priorities cited by member countries include the need for migrants to learn the host country's language and the need for easier access to the local labour market (OECD, 2015).

Lastly, figures for the qualifications held by Montreal residents aged 25 to 64 (Figure 2.6) show that the proportion of those completing higher education is similar to that seen in Toronto and Vancouver, and greater than the average for Quebec. In this category, the proportion of students completing more protracted courses of study (degree/*baccalauréat* or higher) is lower in Montreal (29.6%) than in Toronto (36.7%) and Vancouver (34.1%). So Montreal's students seem to opt mostly for higher education of short duration. And the proportion of persons with no higher education diploma is greater in Montreal (12.4%) than in Toronto (9.9%) and Vancouver (8.4%).

Figure 2.6. **Educational attainment of the population aged 25-64, 2011**

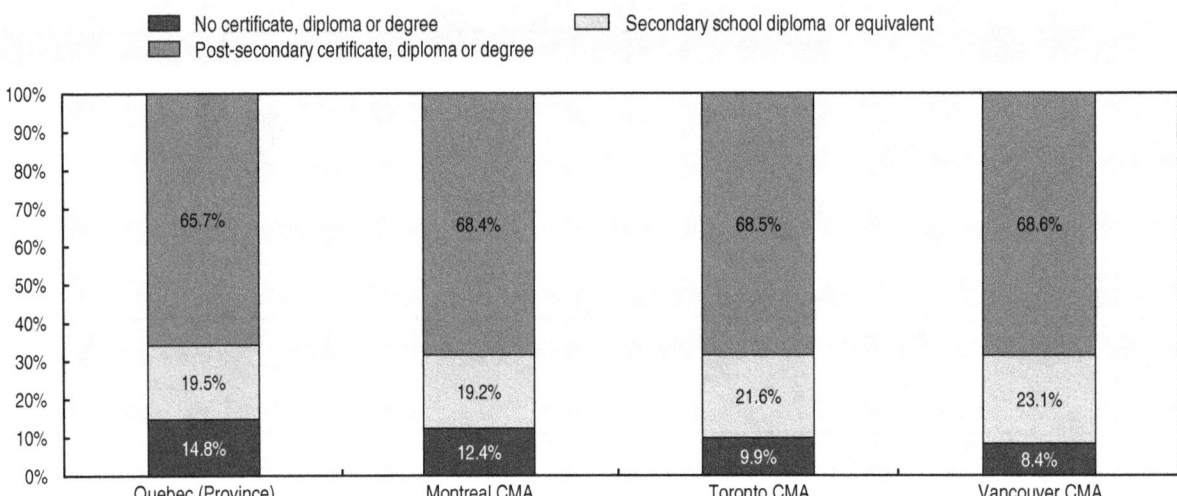

Source: Statistics Canada, 2011 National Household Survey.

A recent study by the *Institut du Québec* (IdQ, 2015) confirms that Montreal lags behind in terms of the educational level of its population. This study points out, however, that the position in Montreal is improving, in that its 25 to 34-year-olds are better educated than 25 to 64-year-olds in a comparison with other similar cities in North America.

There was a marked improvement in the graduation rate[1] between 2009 and 2014; this rose from 67.7% to 76%, close to the target of 77% by 2020 set by the Quebec Ministry of Education. The school dropout rate has fallen significantly in recent years but was still 20.8% in 2013 (24.6% in 2009), well above the Quebec average (16%). That means that nearly 2 500 young Montrealers left school this year without a qualification. Sizeable local disparities can be seen within the Island of Montreal, and some districts in Montreal East have school dropout rates of over 25%.

In sum, the figures on the availability of labour and skills in Montreal's local economy present a constracted picture. Quebec's largest city unquestionably has the capacity to train and attract talent, but that capacity does not seem to be fully reflected in the population's educational attaintment figures. The challenges of retaining talented people and of school dropout rates go some way towards explaining this paradox. Employers may have a plentiful supply of labour because of the city's unquestionable demographic dynamism, driven by immigration, but the skills level of this workforce does not appear to give any clear competitive advantage to the local economy at present.

Productive capacity

The Montreal metropolitan area is the principal driver of the Quebec economy, accounting for 53.5% of GDP in 2014, and a hefty 57% in the services sector. In 2013, Montreal provided 10.5% of Canada's GDP, compared with 11.5% in 2000.

In terms of GDP per capita, Montreal was ranked low in 2012 compared with the other large OECD cities, and well below the levels for Toronto and Vancouver (Figure 2.7).

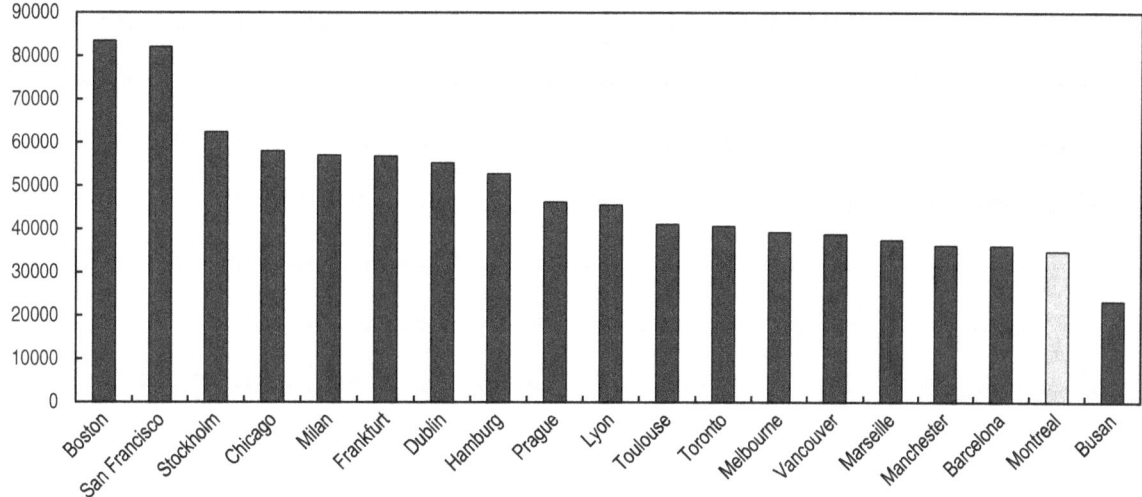

Figure 2.7. **GDP per capita (USD 2010), 2012**

Source: OECD (2016), "Metropolitan areas", OECD Regional Statistics (database), http://dx.doi.org/10.1787/data-00531-en.

Between 2000 and 2012, per capita GDP for Montreal went up very little (by 2.9%) compared with other OECD cities such as Boston, San Francisco, Chicago, Vancouver, Stockholm, Busan and Prague (Figure 2.8).

This finding of relatively low dynamism in the local economy as a whole is explained by the level of labour productivity (ratio of gross domestic product to the number of people in employment); in 2012, this was amongst the lowest of all the OECD cities selected for this study (Figure 2.9). Between 2001 and 2012, labour productivity grew by only 0.1% a year on average, a poorer rate of growth than in Toronto (up 0.2%) and Vancouver (up 0.8%), which means that Montreal ranks 15th out of the 19 OECD cities selected. Over the same period, the North American cities of San Francisco (with average annual growth of 1.9%), Boston (with 1.5%) or Chicago (with 1.0%) recorded far higher rates of growth in labour productivity. It would appear that poor levels of education and capital spending on equipment and R&D, identified in 2004 as some of the chief factors explaining the productivity differential

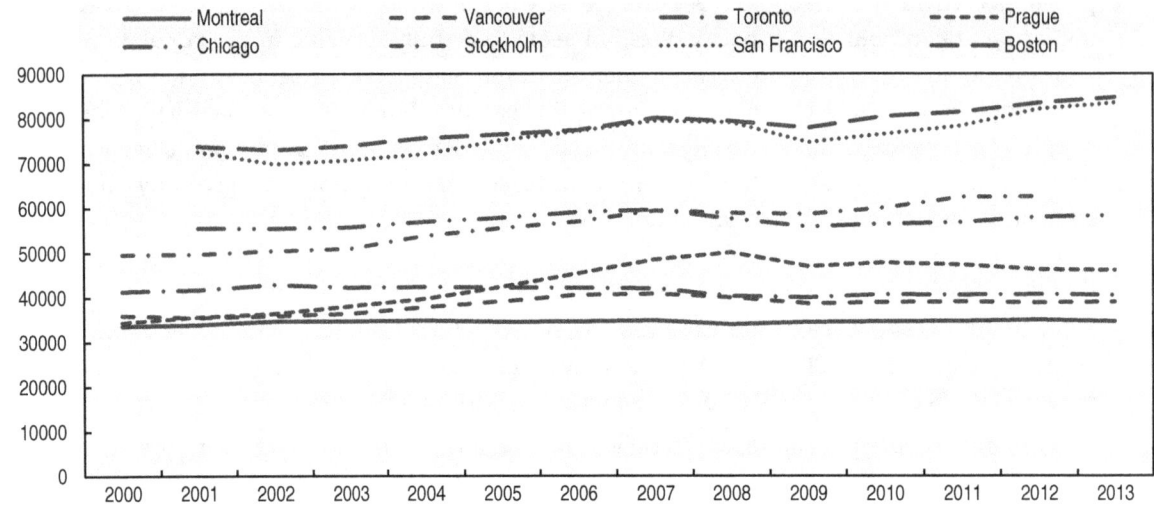

Figure 2.8. **GDP per capita (USD 2010), 2000-13***

* Data not available in 2000 for Boston, Chicago and San Francisco, and in 2013 for Stockholm.
Source: OECD (2016), "Metropolitan areas", OECD Regional Statistics (database), http://dx.doi.org/10.1787/data-00531-en.

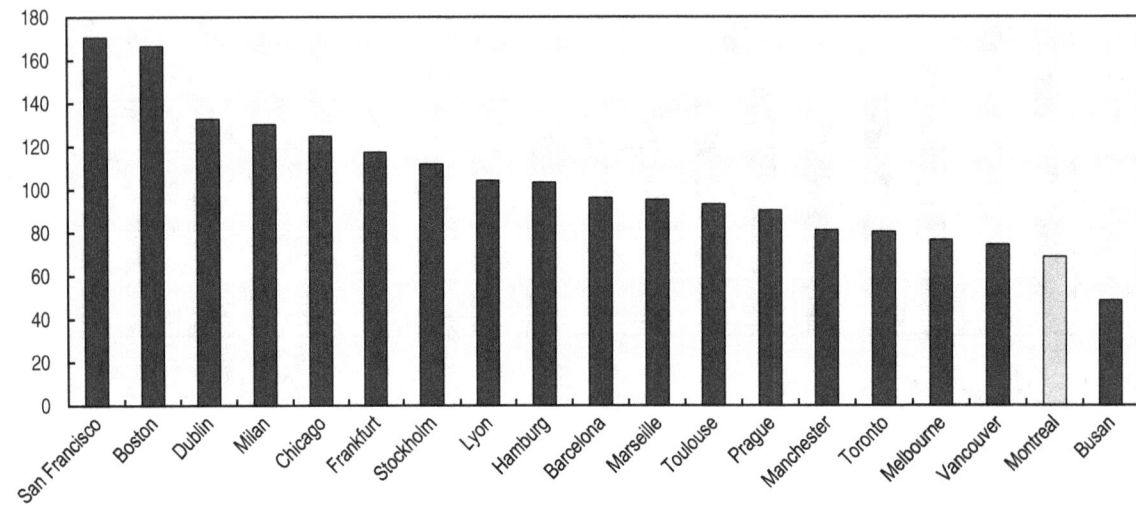

Figure 2.9. **Labour productivity (thousand USD 2010), 2012**

Source: OECD (2016), "Metropolitan areas", OECD Regional Statistics (database), http://dx.doi.org/10.1787/data-00531-en.

between Montreal and the other large cities in the OECD countries (OECD, 2004), are still a major challenge for Montreal today.

The Montreal economy has performed only modestly in recent times, but it is appropriate to distinguish between different sectors of activity, because some have boomed in terms both of jobs (Figure 2.10) and value creation (Table 2.2), whilst others have shown a decline.

In 2014, the sectors of trade (33 7000 jobs, up 21% since 2001) and health care and social assistance (268 000 jobs, up 46% since 2001) were the main providers of employment, followed by manufacturing (224 000 jobs). This latter sector has lost a significant number of jobs since 2001 (down 29%), in contrast to the professional, scientific and technical services sector where the number of jobs rose by 40% over the same period.

Figure 2.10. **Employment by sector of activity, Montreal, 2014**

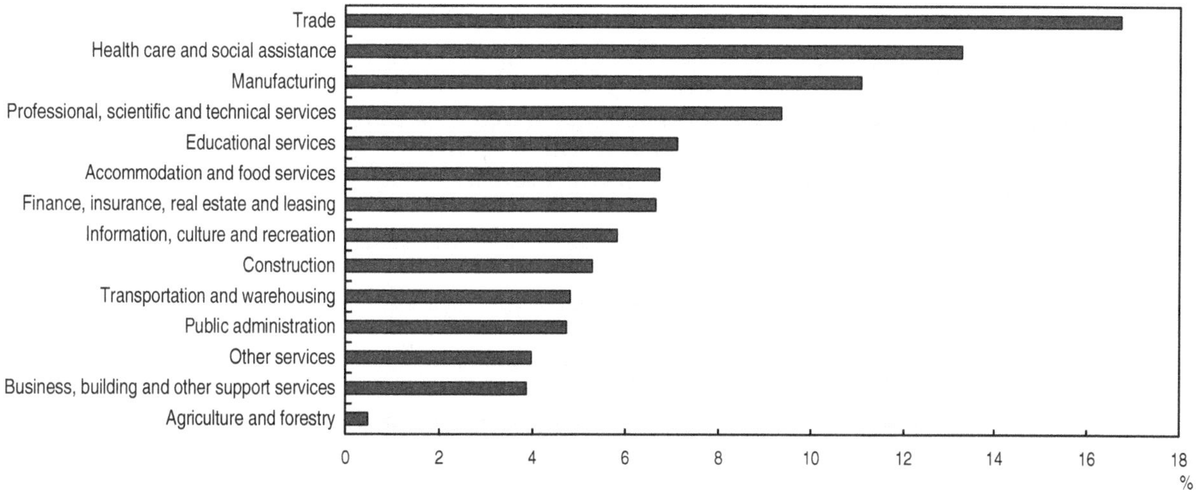

Sector	%
Trade	~17
Health care and social assistance	~13
Manufacturing	~11
Professional, scientific and technical services	~9
Educational services	~7
Accommodation and food services	~7
Finance, insurance, real estate and leasing	~7
Information, culture and recreation	~6
Construction	~5
Transportation and warehousing	~5
Public administration	~5
Other services	~4
Business, building and other support services	~4
Agriculture and forestry	<1

Source: Statistics Canada, Table 282-0131 – Labour Force Survey.

Table 2.2. **Changes in sectoral shares in GDP, Montreal**

	Share of total GDP of Montreal		Growth of sector's share of GDP 2007-13 %	Share in Quebec (2013) %
	2007 %	2013 %		
All industries	/	/	18.4	53.5
Goods-producing sector	24.8	23.1↓	10.1	44.9
Manufacturing (total)	15.4	12.9↓	-0.8	51.4
– Transport equipment	2.9	3.1↑	27.7	84.4
– Food products	1.3	1.2↓	7.1	45.0
– Chemicals	1.6	1.5↓	7.3	74.7
Services sector	75.2	76.9↑	21.1	56.7
Finance and insurance, real estate	19.0	19.9↑	23.8	58.9
Professional, scientific and technical services	6.6	7.6↑	35.4	69.5
Health care and social assistance	7.5	7.9↑	24.0	50.3
Public administration	5.5	5.9↑	27.7	40.5

Source: Data compiled by the Quebec Institute of Statistics (ISQ), Economic Statistics Directorate.

Sectoral changes in terms of GDP (Table 2.2) show that Montreal, like most other large OECD cities, has experienced a shift towards the services sector (76.9% of GDP in 2013). The goods-producing sector remains important, however (23.1% of GDP in 2013). Although there is a declining trend in manufacturing overall (it dropped from 15.4% to 12.9% of GDP between 2007 and 2013), some of these activities continue to show strong growth, notably transport equipment manufacturing (the sector's share of GDP grew by 27.7% between 2007 and 2013). Over the same period, the more traditional manufacturing activities such as the manufacture of food products (up 7.1%) and chemicals (up 7.3%) remained relatively dynamic. Other sectors making a significant contribution to the GDP of Montreal include "health care and social assistance", "finance, insurance and real estate", "professional, scientific and technical services" and "public administration".

Concerning the dynamism of the fabric of small and medium-sized enterprises (SMEs), enterprises with 1-499 employees,[2] in 2014 18.3% of Montreal SMEs reported average annual growth of over 10% in their sales during the previous three years, compared with

20.8% for Toronto and 20.4% for Vancouver and Canada as a whole (Statistics Canada, 2015). But the proportion of SMEs experiencing negative sales growth over the same period is greater in Montreal (15.7%) than in Canada as a whole (11.5%).

In 2014, the two main obstacles to growth cited by Montreal SMEs were fiercer competition (24.2%) and fluctuations in consumer demand (23.7%). Compared with SMEs in Toronto, Vancouver and Canada as a whole, Montreal SMEs more frequently mention government regulations and business taxation rates as factors which hamper their growth. By contrast, they complain relatively less of labour-related problems.

The level of SME internationalisation has risen in Montreal in recent years, with the proportion of small exporters rising from 13.2% in 2011 to 16.2% in 2014 (Statistics Canada, 2015). This proportion was greater in Toronto (18.5%), the same in Vancouver (16.2%), and smaller in Canada as a whole (11.8%). Montreal SMEs that had announced their intention to expand into new markets in 2014 (by 44%, as against 59.6% and 53.3% in the case of Toronto and Vancouver) focused their efforts to a greater extent on the European market (7.5%, as against Toronto 6.9% and Vancouver 5.9%) and to a lesser extent on Asian markets (3.0%, as against Toronto 5.3% and Vancouver 5.1%).

The figures for SME spending in Canada (Statistics Canada, 2011) show that Montreal SMEs are making consistent investments in the area of research and development (R&D), new materials and equipment, new ICT, and staff education and training. It seems, however, that these investments are, for the most part, made by a small number of SMEs which have grown to a relatively large size. When we look at the *median* for SME spending, we find that investment by Montreal SMEs in new materials and equipment (CAD 7 000) is less than the figure for Canada as a whole (CAD 12 000). This underinvestment was highlighted by the OECD back in the early 2000s as one of the main factors accounting for the low productivity of Montreal's workforce (OECD, 2004). Median investment in R&D, on the other hand, is higher than that of SMEs in Toronto, Vancouver, and Canada as a whole. Spending on ICT and staff education and training is similar for SMEs in Montreal and Canada as a whole. On the matter of staff training by SMEs, two surveys conducted by Statistics Canada in 2002 (Statistics Canada, 2004) and 2008 (Statistics Canada, 2009) flagged up inadequacies in this area.

Innovation in Montreal

Innovation, whether technology-related or not, relies heavily on skills. So organisations seeking to develop new strategies for their product markets or to introduce a new technology into their production processes must be able to avail themselves of the technical and organisational skills of their workforce and their partners. But innovation creates in its turn a new need for skills within organisations because it requires the workforce to adapt to a new technology, a new product or a new process.

A number of indicators can be used to record, if only in part, innovation-related activities in Montreal. In order to compare Montreal with other Canadian regions or with other countries, we need to use primarily quantitative data. More qualitative data on initiatives taken to promote and develop the ecosystem of innovation actors in Montreal will be presented in Chapter 3 of this study.

The *Institut du Québec* recently conducted a study which compares Montreal with 14 other North American cities, including Toronto and Vancouver in Canada. Montreal comes in 11th for innovation, on the basis of a set of results for four indicators. In detail: Montreal is ranked fourth in terms of the proportion of its workforce employed in jobs in promising sectors of the future; ninth for the number of STEM (science, technology, engineering, mathematics) graduates per 100 000 head of population; ninth too for the number of agreements in respect of venture capital investments, but last but one for the average value of these agreements.

The IdQ study also points to a low number of patents filed per 100 000 population, Montreal coming bottom of the list of the North American cities looked at in the study. But OECD data available at city level for the year 2008 cast doubt on this finding, since these show Montreal in ninth place among the 10 OECD cities selected for the report, ahead of Vancouver and Toronto (Figure 2.11). The figures for the US cities of San Francisco, Boston and Chicago are higher, admittedly, but Montreal scores better in this regard than Milan, Melbourne, Barcelona or even Manchester.

Figure 2.11. **PCT patent applications per 10 000 inhabitants, 2008**

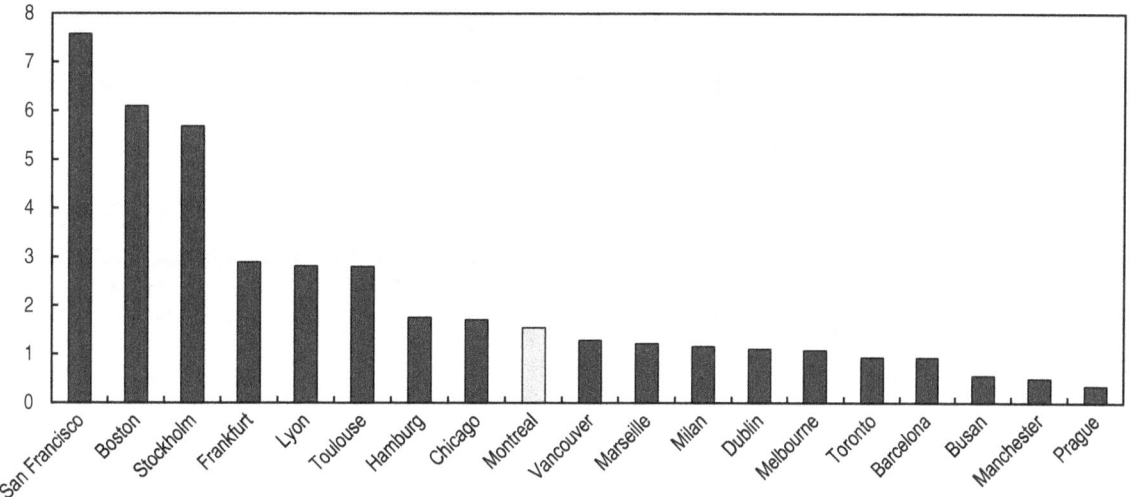

Source: OECD (2016), "Metropolitan areas", OECD Regional Statistics (database), http://dx.doi.org/10.1787/data-00531-en.

Regarding innovation by SMEs (Statistics Canada, 2015), between 2011 and 2014, the proportion of Montreal SMEs that claimed to have committed to at least one type of innovative activity during the past three years rose from 32.4% to 42.4%, a greater increase than in Toronto (up from 40.4% to 47.2%) and Canada as a whole (up from 37.8% to 41.6%), whilst in Vancouver the proportion of innovative SMEs fell (from 41.7% to 39%). Figure 2.12 shows the proportion of innovative SMEs by type of innovation. Montreal's SMEs are relatively well placed in innovation concerning products or services processes and marketing. In organisational innovation, however, they are less active than SMEs in Toronto, Vancouver and Canada as a whole, possibly because the economic fabric of Montreal includes a large number of micro-enterprises.

In 2011, the main reason overwhelmingly given by Montreal SMEs for not making any innovations was that the business had no need to innovate (67.2%). This was a far higher proportion than for SMEs in Toronto (40.4%), Vancouver (48%) and Canada as a whole (49.7%). Lack of trained staff was also cited relatively more often by Montreal SMEs (4% compared with 1.7% for Canada as a whole). There was little mention of lack of financing, which did not seem to be a major obstacle to innovation.

The Statistics Canada Survey of Innovation by Canadian SMEs identifies typical characteristics of innovative enterprises.[3] Thus there is a positive correlation between

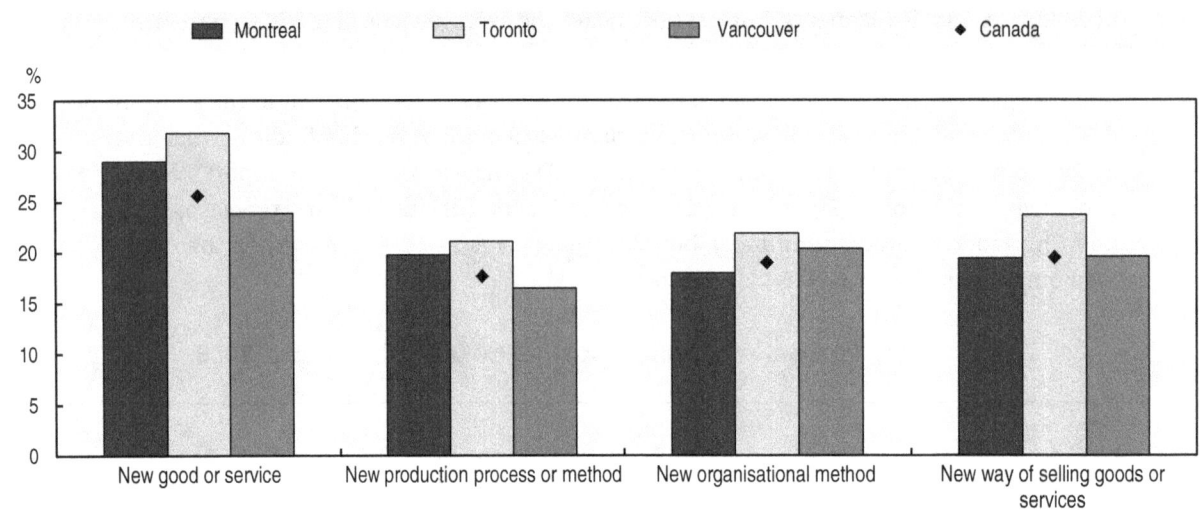

Figure 2.12. **Innovation by Canadian SMEs in the past three years (percentage of SMEs surveyed), 2014**

Source: Statistics Canada (2015), Survey on Financing and Growth of Small and Medium Enterprises, 2014.

innovation and SME size, whether or not they export, and their rate of growth. Another factor is the age of the SME – enterprises started less than 10 years ago are more innovative than older SMEs. As stated earlier, Montreal SMEs tend to be less dynamic and to export less than those based in Toronto.

This survey also shows that certain characteristics of the person in charge of the business, such as age, qualifications and birth abroad, seem to have a considerable effect on an SME's propensity to innovate. Thus SMEs headed by someone younger than 30 are, on average, more innovative, and likewise those where the boss has a college/CEGEP/trade school diploma. According to this survey, businesses headed by someone born abroad tend to innovate more than those whose boss is Canadian-born. It should be noted here that a larger proportion of the Toronto and Vancouver population is foreign-born compared with that of Montreal, which may work against Montreal in terms of innovation.

The Compendium of Science and Technology Indicators published by the Quebec Institute of Statistics (ISQ, 2014) provides a data series that focuses on research and development (R&D) activity. The ISQ uses the Frascati Manual for this compilation. Although, strictly speaking, innovation and R&D are two separate things, they often go together to a greater or lesser degree. R&D happens downstream of the process, potentially leading to the bringing to market of products or services often covered by an intellectual property right.

The R&D data for Quebec are not broken down by region, but they point to quite a sharp fall in overall spending on R&D between 2003 and 2013, whether by government, business and industry or academe. The ratio of R&D to GDP was about 2.75% in 2003, but dropped to 2.25% in 2013. Some countries, including Finland, Sweden, Japan, Denmark, the USA and Germany, are clearly ahead of Quebec and Canada in this regard, and did not experience the same slow-down in R&D effort during the review period. The adverse economic climate most certainly affected this spending pattern, because the point of inflexion occurs around 2007. Since then, the downward trend has continued, with slow recovery and budgetary stringency on the part of public administrations. But other countries have responded differently to the same economic constraints.

Tax credits for R&D by the private sector are also down in Quebec over the same period. There was a fall in both the number of beneficiary enterprises (6 800 in 2012 as against 8 000 or so in 2008) and the amounts concerned (CAD 550 million in 2012 as against CAD 725 million in 2008). The data also show that the overwhelming majority of these tax benefits are given essentially to a small number of very big companies in a small number of industries. And these Quebec companies, most of them large and operating chiefly in a group of industries such as aerospace, are strongly represented in Montreal. The fall-off in tax credits reflects the fact that businesses are spending less, not that government fiscal policy has changed.

Growth in the number of scientific and technical writings published in Quebec is amongst the world's best (ISQ, 2014). University publications dominate the list, and especially those on health and the life sciences. It is reasonable to suppose that Montreal's input is considerable, given that it has four universities.

The data for production and innovation capability in Montreal prompt a number of findings. Over the past 15 years, Montreal's economy overall has been relatively sluggish, and labour productivity has tended to stagnate. But this conceals major changes that have significantly impacted on the fabric of the local economy. Whilst the share of goods-producing sectors remains relatively large, making for diversity and resilience in the local economy, the great majority of job creation is in the services sector. More specifically, five sectors currently account for nearly three-quarters of all jobs created: professional, scientific and technical services; health care and social assistance; finance, insurance, real estate and leasing; business, building and other support services; accommodation and food services (*Emploi-Québec*, n.d.). The labour market is thus polarised between jobs requiring a post-secondary diploma (college or university), which are about 80% of new jobs, and low-grade jobs that do not pay well and require few or no qualifications. Because the business fabric consists chiefly of very small firms with little growth, no innovation and operating only locally, the creation of quality jobs is bound to be limited. In 2011, the proportion of jobs requiring intermediate or high skills was only 35%, lower than in Toronto (39%).[4] But the presence of a number of fast-growing and innovative SMEs which export, and of large multinational groupings able to rely on instruments like patents which protect innovation, and on a lively scientific community, means that the Montreal economy possesses major assets for innovation and the creation of quality jobs.

Challenges for the labour market

Labour market indicators can give a better picture of how the balance between the skills of the population and production capabilities in Montreal expresses itself in terms of jobs.

The Montreal metropolitan area is, first of all, one with a high labour force participation rate (ratio of the number of persons participating in the labour market – employed and unemployed – to the working-age population aged 15-64). In 2014, Montreal ranked seventh out of the 19 OECD cities selected (Figure 2.13).

The size of Montreal's pool of labour was one of the main factors which made the city competitive in the early 2000s (OECD, 2004), but the labour force participation rate has fallen steadily over the past 10 years (from 81% in 2004 to 77.3% in 2014), a trend also seen in Toronto, Vancouver and Chicago. At the same time, the rate in cities like Hamburg, Frankfurt, Milan, Stockholm or San Francisco has risen steeply.

Unemployment in Montreal is higher, at 8.7% for the third quarter of 2015, than in Quebec as a whole (7.8%) and Canada as a whole (7%). This may be due in part to the

Figure 2.13. **Participation rate, 2014**

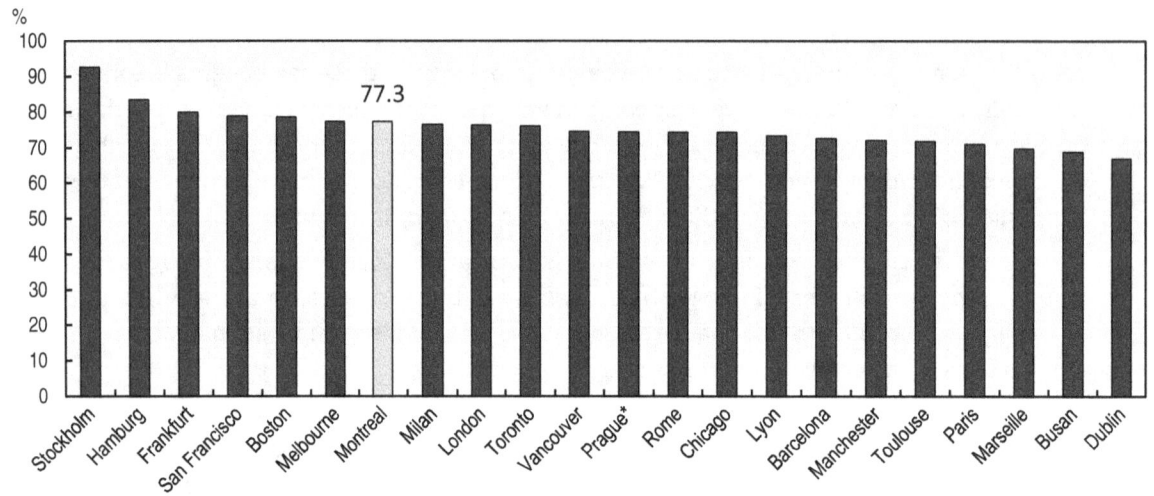

* Data available for Prague in 2013.
Source: OECD (2016), "Metropolitan areas", OECD Regional Statistics (database), http://dx.doi.org/10.1787/data-00531-en.

disproportionately high rate of unemployment amongst the immigrant population (11.3% in 2014) and to major job losses in manufacturing, where it is difficult to find new employment for people made redundant (FGM, 2015).

Figure 2.14 below shows that there is a problem absorbing immigrants into the Montreal labour market: unemployment among recent immigrants is far higher here than in Toronto, Vancouver and the average for Canada. Moreover, immigrants seem to have difficulty becoming part of the labour market over the longer term, since unemployment amongst immigrants who arrived over 10 years ago remains higher than amongst native-born Canadians, which is not the case in Toronto, Vancouver and in Canada generally.

Figure 2.14. **Comparison of unemployment rates for immigrant and Canadian-born populations, 2014**

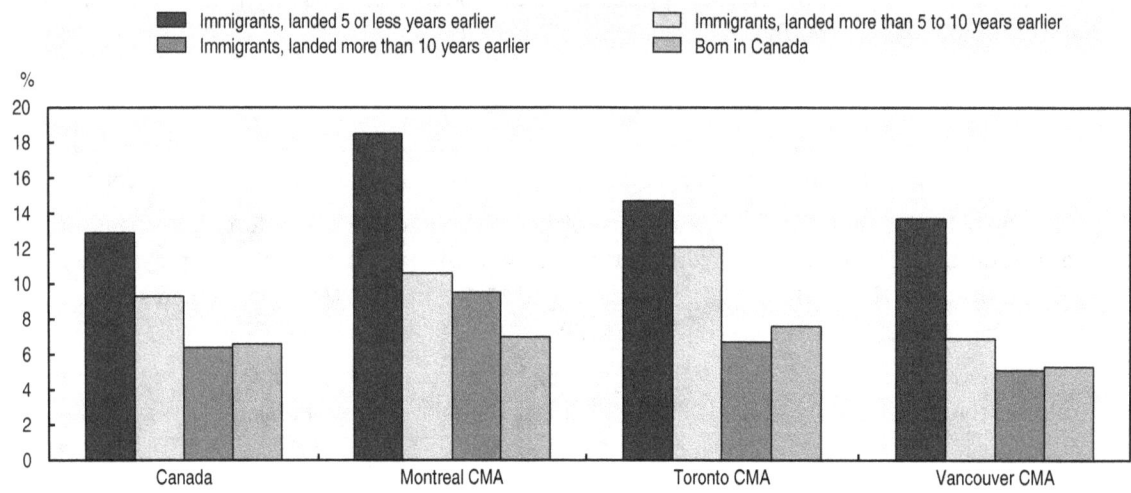

Source: Statistics Canada, Table 282-0101 – Labour Force Survey.

However, compared against the other OECD cities, Montreal came in 19th for the percentage of jobless persons in the labour force in 2013 (Figure 2.15).

Figure 2.15. **Share of unemployed people in the labour force, 2013**

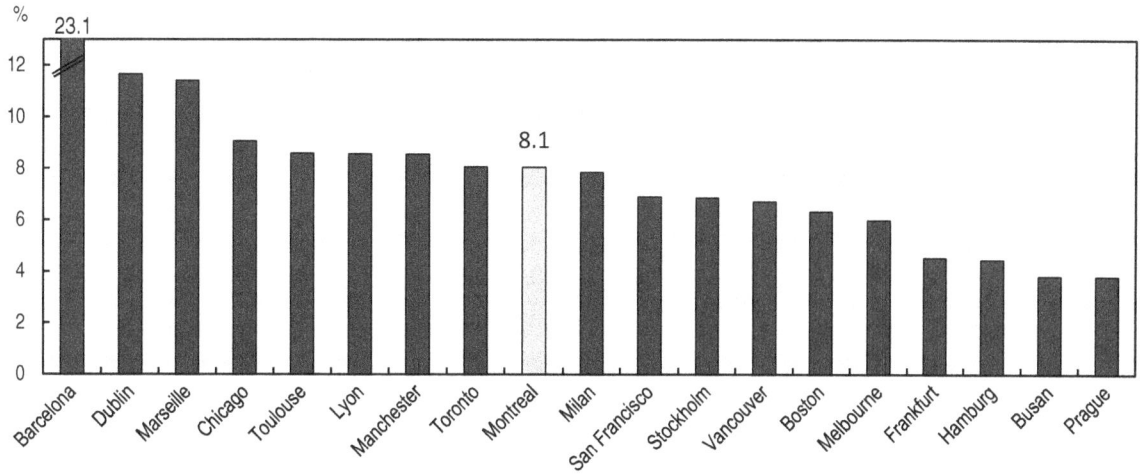

Source: OECD (2016), "Metropolitan areas", OECD Regional Statistics (database), http://dx.doi.org/10.1787/data-00531-en.

The local labour market in Montreal does not appear sensitive to the economic climate, since unemployment levels fluctuated very little during the period 2000-14 (between 7.3% and 9.6%). Comparison with a selection of North American cities (Figure 2.16) illustrates this: prior to the 2008 crisis, joblessness in Montreal was broadly higher than in the other cities studied. Between 2008 and 2010, cities like San Francisco, Chicago and Toronto saw their unemployment rates shoot up, higher than the rate in Montreal. But in recent years, unemployment has fallen back more significantly in these other cities than in Montreal, so that unemployment there was once again the highest in 2014.

Figure 2.16. **Share of unemployed people in the labour force,
selected North American cities, 2000-14**

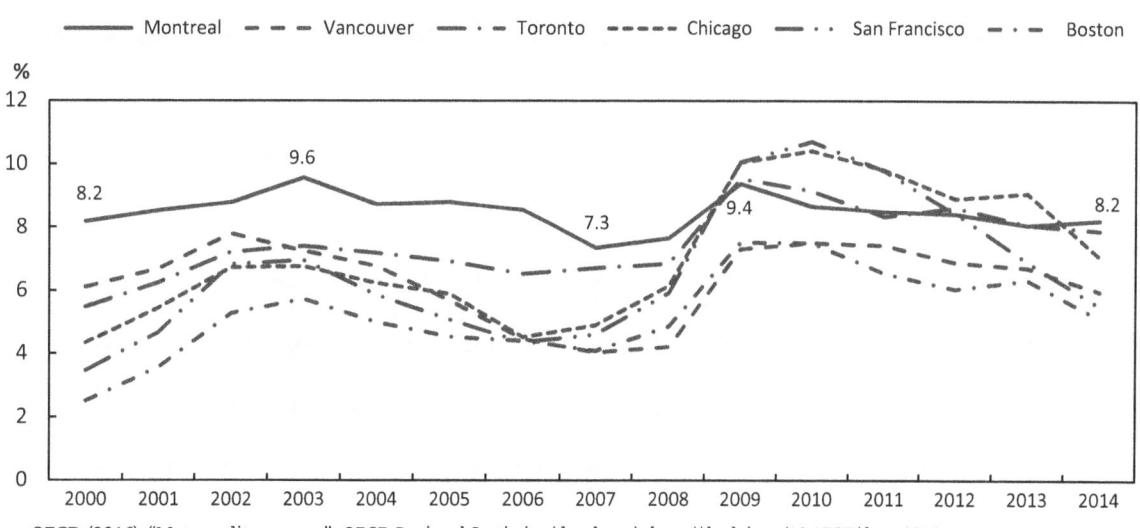

Source: OECD (2016), "Metropolitan areas", OECD Regional Statistics (database), http://dx.doi.org/10.1787/data-00531-en.

The OECD skills diagnostic tool enables us to analyse the adequacy of the match between supply and demand in a region or a city, but it is also interesting to see to what extent people in employment have a level of qualifications that corresponds to the skills needed for the post they hold. Boudarbat and Montmarquette (2013) found the rate of over-qualification in the Montreal metropolitan area to be 32% in 2011, similar to that seen in Toronto and Vancouver. This phenomenon does not affect all employees in the same way. For example, holders of a trade school diploma are more likely to be in a job which does not match their qualifications. This is because the percentage of persons graduating from these establishments has increased in recent years whilst the proportion of jobs needing this type of training has tended to decrease. These data bear out the importance of efforts to achieve a better match between the skills that individuals build up and the needs of Montreal's economy.

Some conclusions on the strengths and weaknesses of Montreal's economy

Montreal unquestionably has the capacity to train and attract talent, being home to high-calibre higher education and research establishments. The city continues to exhibit a certain demographic dynamism, thanks to international immigration, so the local economy can rely on a plentiful supply of labour. Labour force participation in Montreal is amongst the highest for the OECD cities analysed. The economic fabric of Montreal is diversified, as shown by the presence of structured industrial clusters in a range of high value-added sectors. The services sector is by far the leading provider of employment, but the goods-producing sector is still relatively important and includes fast-growing areas of excellence in aerospace, the life sciences, medical technology and video games.

Nevertheless, a number of elements are indicative of weaknesses in the Montreal economy. The potential offered by education and training does not seem to be fully reflected in the qualifications of the population, which limits the pool of skills available to the local economy. This limited availability of skills is matched by a relatively poor dynamism of production activities, which means that economic actors do not show a high demand for skills. Compared with the OECD cities selected for this study, the Montreal metropolitan area has low per capita GDP and low productivity, and these two indicators have remained virtually stagnant for the past 15 years.

The fact that the fabric of the economy includes a majority of micro-enterprises which are not innovative and focus only on the local market goes some way towards explaining why the local economy is relatively sluggish. Recovery from the economic crisis of 2008 brought sizeable job creation, but those jobs were mainly in low value-added sectors such as trade and health care and social assistance. As in other OECD cities, the local labour market thus tends to be polarised between quality jobs in high value-added sectors, indicative of transition towards a knowledge-based economy, and lower-grade jobs requiring few or no qualifications. As a result, individuals with only an intermediate-level qualification have less chance of finding a job commensurate with their skills and are often overqualified. Thus there is a risk that competition for low-skilled jobs will become fiercer, potentially pushing down the quality of these jobs in terms of pay, security and opportunities for career advancement and squeezing the least qualified out of the labour market.

The main labour market indicators show that structural unemployment in the Montreal metropolitan area is high compared with the other North American cities but has remained relatively stable in recent years. Getting young people and immigrants into work, retaining the most highly skilled, and reducing school dropout rates, are major issues for Montreal.

The table which follows presents, for each of the indicators considered, a relative assessment of Montreal's performance. Depending on the availability of data for each indictor, Montreal is compared with other metropolitan areas in the country (Canada), with selected metropolitan areas in North America, or with metropolitan areas in the rest of the world (taken from a selection of reference metropolitan areas*).

Table 2.3. **Comparative assessment of the Montreal metropolitan area**

Subject	Indicators	Level of analysis*	Comparative assessment
Demographic characteristics	Population growth	OECD metropolitan areas	○
	Old-age dependency ratio	OECD metropolitan areas	▲
Educational level	Level of qualification	Canada	▲
Economy	Per capita GDP	OECD metropolitan areas	■
	Labour productivity	OECD metropolitan areas	■
SMEs	Spending on new ICT	Canada	▲
	Spending on staff education and training	Canada	▲
	Spending on R&D	Canada	○
	Spending on new materials and equipment	Canada	■
	Internationalisation	Canada	▲
Innovation	Patent applications	OECD metropolitan areas	▲
	Innovation by SMEs	Canada	■
Labour market	Participation	OECD metropolitan areas	○
	Unemployment	OECD metropolitan areas	▲
	Youth unemployment	Canada	■
	Getting immigrants into work	Canada	■

* Assessment at the OECD analysis level looked at the following metropolitan areas: Barcelona, Boston, Busan, Chicago, Dublin, Frankfurt, Hamburg, Lyon, Manchester, Marseille, Melbourne, Milan, Prague, San Francisco, Stockholm, Toronto, Toulouse and Vancouver.
Assessment at the Canada analysis level covered the census metropolitan areas of Toronto and Vancouver, plus data for Canada as a whole.
Assessment at the North American metropolitan areas analysis level covered the metropolitan areas of Toronto, Vancouver, Chicago, Boston and San Francisco.
○: Montreal's performance is amongst the best for the areas selected.
▲: Montreal's performance is average amongst the areas selected.
■: Montreal's performance is amongst the least good for the areas selected.

Notes

1. The graduation rate measures the proportion of young people obtaining a high school diploma (DES) or diploma of vocational studies (DEP), or other qualification, no more than 7 years after starting their first year of secondary education.

2. The data used are drawn from the Survey on Financing and Growth of Small and Medium Enterprises for 2011 and 2014. Following a change to the questionnaire, data on spending and obstacles to innovation were not collected in 2014.

3. The innovative character of a business is defined here on the basis of self-reporting by the enterprise and not on objective indicators such as number of patents filed.

4. Statistics Canada, CANSIM Table 282-0133.

References

Bacolod, M. et al. (2009), "Skills in the City", *Journal of Urban Economics*, Elsevier, Vol. 65, No. 2, March, pp. 136-153.

Berry, C. and E. Glaeser (2005), "The Divergence of Human Capital Levels across Cities", *Regional Science*, Vol. 84, No. 3, pp. 407-444.

Boudarbat, B. and C. Montmarquette (2013). *Origine et sources de la surqualification dans la région métropolitaine de Montréal* [Origins and sources of over-qualification in the Montreal Metropolitan Region], Project Report, Montreal, CIRANO, p. 113.

Emploi-Québec (n.d.), *Portrait de l'emploi et du marché du travail* [Portrait of employment and the labour market], *www.emploiquebec.gouv.qc.ca/regions/montreal/portrait-de-lemploi-et-du-marche-du-travail/*.

FGM, Foundation of Greater Montreal (2015), *Vital Signs, Greater Montreal in Transition.*

Froy, F., S. Giguère and M. Meghnagi (2012), "Skills for Competitiveness: A Synthesis Report", *OECD Local Economic and Employment Development (LEED) Working Papers*, 2012/09, OECD Publishing.

Gordon, D.L.A. and M. Janzen (2013), "Suburban Nation? Estimating the size of Canada's suburban population", *Journal of Architectural and Planning Research*, Vol. 30, No. 3, pp. 197-220.

Institut du Québec (2015), *Comparer Montréal: Tableau de Bord de la Région Métropolitaine de Montréal* [Comparing Montreal: Scoreboard of the Montreal Metropolitan Region], Institut du Québec.

MI and CEM (Montréal International and Metropolitan Employment Council) (2015), *Étude des facteurs associés à la rétention des immigrants temporaires dans le Grand Montréal* [Study of factors associated with the retention of temporary immigrants in Greater Montreal].

Montreal Metropolitan Community (MMC) (2013), *Perspective Grand Montréal* [Perspective of Greater Montreal], *Bulletin de la Communauté Métropolitaine de Montréal*, No. 24.

OECD (2015), *Job Creation and Local Economic Development*, OECD Publishing, Paris, http://dx.doi.org/10.1787/9789264215009-en.

OECD (2014a), *OECD Regional Outlook 2014: Regions and Cities: Where Policies and People Meet*, OECD Publishing, Paris, http://dx.doi.org/10.1787/9789264201415-en.

OECD (2014b), *Employment and Skills Strategies in Canada*, OECD Publishing, Paris, http://dx.doi.org/10.1787/9789264209374-en.

OECD and China Development Research Foundation (2010), *Trends in Urbanisation and Urban Policies in OECD Countries: What Lessons for China?*, OECD Publishing, Paris, http://dx.doi.org/10.1787/9789264092259-en.

OECD (2006), *Competitive Cities in the Global Economy*, OECD Publishing, Paris, http://dx.doi.org/10.1787/9789264027091-en.

OECD (2004), *OECD Territorial Reviews: Montreal, Canada 2004*, OECD Publishing, Paris, http://dx.doi.org/10.1787/9789264105980-en.

OECD (2003), Frascati Manual 2002: Proposed Standard Practice for Surveys on Research and Experimental Development. The Measurement of Scientific and Technological Activities, OECD Publishing, Paris.

Quebec Institute of Statistics (ISQ) (2014), Compendium of Science and Technology Indicators, p. 129.

Statistics Canada (2015), *Survey on Financing and Growth of Small and Medium Enterprises, 2014.*

Statistics Canada (2013), *Sectoral Outlook 2013-2015 – Montreal.*

Statistics Canada (2011), *Survey on Financing and Growth of Small and Medium Enterprises, 2011.*

Statistics Canada (2009), *Access and Support to Education and Training Survey (ASETS)*, http://www23.statcan.gc.ca/imdb/p2SV.pl?Function=getSurvey&SDDS=5151.

Statistics Canada (2004), *Adult Education and Training Survey (AETS)*, http://www23.statcan.gc.ca/imdb-bmdi/instrument/3879_Q1_V2-eng.pdf.

Tochtermann, L. and N. Clayton (2011), *Moving on up, moving on out?* Centre for Cities, London.

Veneri, P. (2015), "Urban Spatial Structure in OECD Cities: Is Urban Population Decentralising or Clustering?", *OECD Regional Development Working Papers*, No. 2015/01, OECD Publishing, Paris, http://dx.doi.org/10.1787/5js3d834r3q7-en.

Chapter 3

Initiatives in Montreal: Key findings

> *This chapter provides an overview of initiatives carried out in the various fields covered by this study and emphasised by the diagnosis made in Chapter 2. It highlights a number of advances and challenges, which are contrasted with other countries' experiences in four fields: i) Co-ordination between employment and skills development policies and economic development policies, and how they are relevant to Montreal; ii) Creation of a productive local economy; iii) Support for entrepreneurship, innovation and economic development; and iv) Ensuring that growth is inclusive.*

The previous chapter explained that, when contrasted with comparable towns across North America, the Montreal economy suffers from a low skills and productivity equilibrium. There are weaknesses both in its productive capacity and productivity, and in its supply of skills. Montreal has high-quality education institutions, a booming research sector and considerable appeal for international talent. It has a diverse economic fabric consisting of high value-added, structured industrial clusters. However, its potential for mobilising talent is not fully reflected in the qualifications of the population. While some innovative Montreal-based entrepreneurs deliberately choose not to follow a conventional model of business growth in order to preserve a degree of versatility and autonomy, a majority of micro-enterprises appear, by contrast, to lack ambition; with little innovation, for example, in their organisation of work, focusing only on the local market. The local labour market tends to be polarised between premium jobs in high value-added sectors and lower quality jobs requiring few qualifications. As a result, part of the workforce is overqualified and another supplanted, contributing to high structural unemployment in the city.

Initiatives should target both local productive capacity and the supply of skills so as to place Montreal on a trajectory aimed at a high skills and productivity equilibrium that can create more and better quality jobs. These initiatives cover a wide range of sectors ranging from education, training and employment to innovation and entrepreneurship. Of course, not all of these priority areas fall within the remit of the municipality of Montreal. However, they may require a targeted approach and a degree of coherence and integration involving all levels of government. In this connection, current discussions on special metropolis status for Montreal are timely.

In order to identify initiatives to be strengthened or established with a view to steering Montreal towards a high skills and productivity equilibrium that can create more quality jobs, public policies already in place must first be evaluated. It is therefore essential to analyse initiatives that may have an impact on productive capacity and the supply of skills, whether implemented by the city authorities or by other stakeholders, or at government level, and to compare them with the result of international experience. To this end, the OECD has identified a number of aspects of the intervention framework that may help to set a local economy on a path towards a high skills and productivity equilibrium.

This chapter presents the key findings of a study that analysed policies and initiatives conducted in the Montreal area on employment, skills development and innovation by the various actors. Using a series of indicators, it will set out the strengths and weaknesses of the current public policy framework in four key areas. Box 3 below explains the methodology used.

Figure 3.1 shows all of the results from the indicator scoreboard. It highlights the unevenness of public policies implemented by several actors at federal, provincial, regional and municipal level. Despite recent efforts to streamline public policy and interaction between these actors with a view to improving co-ordination of their initiatives and avoiding duplications and inconsistencies, the harmonisation of strategies and initiatives

> Box 3. **Tool for evaluating the public policy framework in Montreal**
>
> The OECD LEED programme identified a set of best practices in employment, skills development and innovation policy in order to evaluate the public policy framework in four key areas:
>
> 1. Co-ordination between employment, skills development and economic development policies, and how they are relevant to Montreal
>
> 2. Creation of a productive local economy – adding value through skills and avoiding the low skills equilibrium trap
>
> 3. Support for entrepreneurship, innovation and economic development – targeting policies aimed at local employment sectors and investing in job quality
>
> 4. Ensuring that growth is inclusive – leveraging skills and economic development opportunities to promote integration into the labour market
>
> Each of these themes is evaluated in detail on the basis of indicators given a score on a scale of 1 (low) to 5 (high). These scores were calculated based on methodology developed by the OECD, drawing on documentary research and questionnaires completed by service and programme managers at the various administrative levels, as well as supplementary interviews. This methodology has been used by the OECD in a number of studies, including the OECD Reviews on Local Job Creation.
>
> The preliminary results of this exercise were presented and discussed at a round-table discussion held in Montreal in November 2015, bringing together several organisations involved in economic development, skills development and employment at various levels, and representing the public, private and not-for-profit/non-governmental sector.

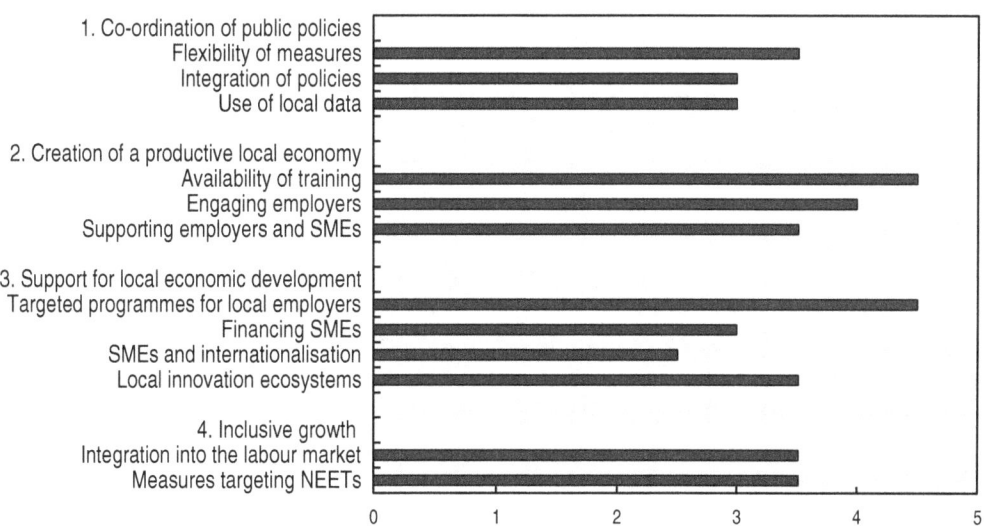

Figure 3.1. **The public policy framework: results from the dashboard**

between the different levels of government nevertheless poses a major challenge in Montreal's institutional context.

The four themes of the study will be presented and discussed successively, accompanied by an explanation of the results and, in some cases, examples describing the situation in Montreal. Examples of initiatives identified in OECD countries will also be included in the analysis in order to draw comparisons.

Theme 1: Improved co-ordination between employment, skills development and economic development policies, and how they are relevant to Montreal

This theme focuses on evaluating the degree of flexibility and co-ordination of public measures, as well as how local data are incorporated during their development. Figure 3.2 shows the results for these three indicators. The aim is to analyse the extent to which public policies are appropriate to the specific conditions observed in Montreal regarding employment, skills and the local economy.

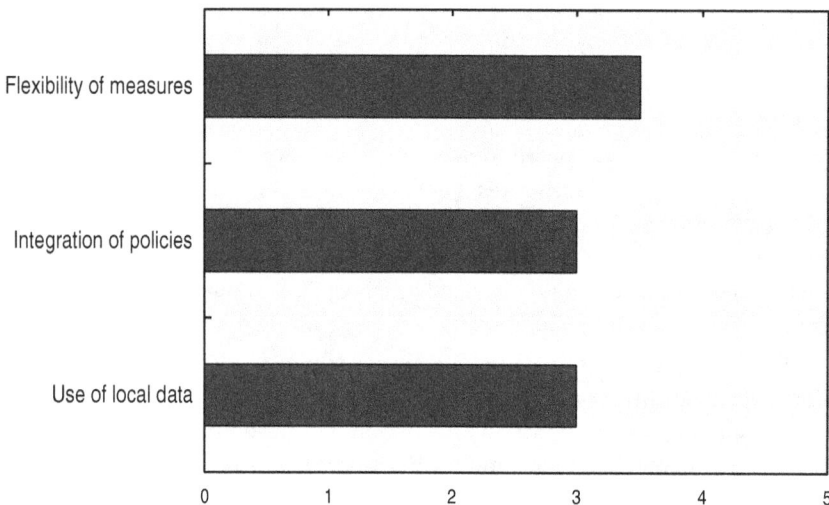

Figure 3.2. **Flexibility, co-ordination and local data**

1.1. Flexibility in the design and implementation of employment and training policies and initiatives

Flexibility has been defined by the OECD as the "the possibility to adjust policy at its various design, implementation and delivery stages to make it better adapted to local contexts, actions carried out by other organisations, strategies being pursued, and challenges and opportunities faced" (Froy and Giguère, 2009). In the context of this study, flexibility refers to the latitude that exists in the management of employment and training systems in Montreal, rather than the flexibility of the labour market itself. The provincial, federal, metropolitan and municipal governments must provide sufficient margin for manoeuvre when allocating responsibilities in the fields of designing policies and programmes, managing budgets, identifying performance targets, setting criteria for eligibility and outsourcing services.

A flexible employment policy framework

Employment and training policies for unemployed people in Montreal are primarily devised at provincial level by the central office of the *Emploi-Québec* public employment service. They consist of universal services accessible to any interested person or organisation, encompassing reception, registration, referral, advice, labour market information (LMI), as well as an online placement service (matching job seekers with job providers). They also include other measures, access to which is determined based on the profile and needs of the individual, and by their employment insurance or welfare contribution status.

The regional branches of *Emploi-Québec*, including the Montreal branch and its 17 local employment centres (CLEs) designed to be used by individuals, enjoy a significant margin of manoeuvre regarding choices of measures to be implemented according to local needs. The regional office in Montreal benefits from an overall budget for services and may deploy resources according to established needs and priorities, while respecting this budget. The regional office oversees the negotiation and management of service agreements with external resources, which, in the majority of cases, are non-profit community organisations. However, the CLEs may, in some cases, choose suppliers that will deliver the programmes or influence how they are chosen. Services offered under these contracts are based on expected results in terms of target customer volumes and the results of the interventions (returning to work, returning to college, etc.), the broad parameters of which are set by *Emploi-Québec* at provincial level.

Emploi-Québec's website, which includes a section for Montreal, is publicly available, and CLEs are accessible to any interested person. Centres offering access to a number of different services are open to all, allowing use of various job search tools and providing information on the labour market and training, local businesses and other job search resources and assistance. Staff running these centres advise users and guide them towards more specialist services if necessary. There are essentially two types of users: firstly, people who come to obtain temporary or permanent income support, depending on their situation; and secondly, those seeking career guidance, which involves establishing a personalised pathway that is drawn up by the individual and their CLE adviser.

Emploi-Québec offers a range of measures concerning training, preparation for employment, self-employment, wage subsidies, recognition of qualifications, social assistance and aid. The customer and their local branch officer determine together which measures suit each individual case, taking into account the individual's characteristics, their aspirations and aptitudes, as well as the needs of the local labour market. The individual will then be referred to specialist organisations at different stages of their pathway, and they will be monitored throughout this by their *Emploi-Québec* adviser. Budget constraints can, in some cases, impose delays or restrictions on access to certain measures, but this remains rare.

A Regional Council of Labour Market Partners (CRPMT) advises, guides and supports the *Emploi-Québec* regional office. It consists of six employers' representatives, six trade union representatives, two community organisation representatives, four representatives from the training field and the regional director of *Emploi-Québec*. In addition, the regional director of the Ministry of the Economy, Science and Innovation (MESI), as well as a representative from the Ministry of Immigration, Diversity and Inclusion (MIDI) and another from the Ministry of Municipal Affairs and Land Occupancy (MAMOT) participate as non-voting members. Note that no municipal or federal representative sits on the Council.

Beyond the services delivered by the public employment service, training for adults, including training focused on literacy, francisation, English as a second language or vocational training, are offered by the school boards (CS) and general and vocational colleges (CEGEP). The school boards can issue skills training certificates (STC) without ministerial approval for short training courses, and the CEGEPs can produce attestations of college studies (ACS) for short training courses focused on the needs of the labour market. *Emploi-Québec* funds numerous individuals' participation in these training courses.

The school boards have a business assistance service (BAS) in order to meet business needs in terms of employment-based and customised training, while CEGEPs offer a range of

3. INITIATIVES IN MONTREAL: KEY FINDINGS

> **Box 4. The financing of public employment services in Montreal**
>
> Over 80% of the financing of public employment services, including *Emploi-Québec* first and foremost, comes from the federal government. Two main agreements provide the framework for these financial transfers between federal and provincial government. The first, and most significant in terms of the sums involved, called the Labour Market Development Agreement (LMDA), draws from the employment insurance account into which employers and employees pay contributions. Under the LMDA, priority is given to those entitled to employment insurance when it comes to participation in measures that require significant expenditure, such as training. The LMDA also broadly outlines the services and measures the province must establish in order to access federal funding.
>
> The second federal-provincial agreement is called the Canada Job Fund Agreement (CJFA). These additional sums are intended for people who are not entitled to employment insurance, including unemployed people not covered by employment insurance and workers with low levels of schooling. For the most part, the services and measures financed by the CJFA are the same as for the LMDA. Other agreements relate to disabled people and older workers. Finally, the federal government directly manages a number of other programmes, including a Youth Strategy and various initiatives for indigenous populations.
>
> The detailed design of the public employment service, and its implementation, is the responsibility of the province of Quebec. Regional offices and local employment centres thus offer an overall "basket of services", which means that these bodies can opt for different compositions from one site to another, according to local needs. This basket of measures and services is also set out in such a way that it allows for adaptation to local contexts. In addition, around 20% of budgets allocated for public employment services come from the provincial government. The beneficiaries of social welfare constitute a key group for the Government of Quebec, where these individuals are deemed capable of being employed or taking steps in this direction.
>
> Finally, the two governments concurrently offer services providing information on the labour market and matching job seekers with employers (Online Placement in Quebec and the *Guichet Emploi* (job bank) in Canada).
>
> According to the latest comparative data available and published by the OECD, Canada invested the equivalent of 0.23% of its GDP in active measures for the labour market in 2013 (administration, information, preparation for employment, stabilising employment, placement, training, employment and self-employment subsidies, as well as other measures), i.e. less than half of the average of the OECD countries (0.56%) and around half of what the country invested in this domain in 1996 (0.45%).

continuous training for adults who want to develop or update their vocational skills, and for businesses that want to develop or enhance the skills of their workforce. But the prevailing rules and resources allocated do not appear to be sufficient to meet demand, particularly at college level, and the continuous training offer so far appears under-developed.

A centralised and relatively rigid training and education policy framework

As regards young people's basic education, including technical and vocational training, this falls within the remit of the Ministry of Education, Higher Education and Research (MEESR), which is not decentralised in the same way as *Emploi-Québec*. Education is a provincial constitutional responsibility in Canada, and programmes are established by the Ministry, which is also responsible for approving studies. A recent OECD report revealed a lack of flexibility and excessive institutional compartmentalisation of the vocational and technical training and education system in Quebec, limiting the degree of responsiveness to local demand (OECD, 2014). In most cases, school boards and college institutions have little latitude for adapting curricula, syllabuses and training courses to the needs of employers and individuals. The creation of new syllabuses requires approval from the Ministry of Education, and this process generally takes several months to finalise. This lack of flexibility has also been seen in the training offered to adults, which is characterised by strict eligibility criteria that limit possibilities for reintegration and career progression of individuals who have not obtained a secondary school diploma.

There are nevertheless several partnership exercises and efforts to adapt to local contexts, particularly those of the labour market. For example, the MEESR is conducting several consultation exercises with representatives from the world of work in order to develop or adjust programmes or training courses, including apprenticeships, so as to take into account specific needs and the changing realities of the labour market. The MEESR also produces a "*carte des enseignements*" (education card) that grants certain regions authorisations to teach, primarily in vocational and technical training, based on the composition of the area's economic activity.

While the conceptual, strategic and regulatory component, including the approval of studies, is the responsibility of the MEESR, practical management is the remit of the school boards (CS), which are responsible for overseeing primary and secondary teaching establishments, and of the CEGEPs, which offer a technical training component designed to prepare young people for employment linked to this training.

> **Box 5. Examples of flexible education and vocational training systems in Canada (Ontario) and the United States (California and Michigan)**
>
> The OECD has highlighted the importance of having education and vocational training systems that are sufficiently flexible to be capable of responding to the changing needs of local labour markets. A flexible training system can ensure there is a better match between the training offered and the needs of employers, which can promote productivity gains and improve the quality of jobs.
>
> In Ontario, each community college has a programme advisory committee which reports to the president of the college through a board of governors. This committee provides assistance in shaping the content of the programmes, as well as the skills the graduates should acquire. The fact that the committee consists of employers ensures that the programmes are relevant and that any deficiencies in the training courses offered by the college are identified.
>
> In the United States, while governance systems in education and vocational training differ depending on the state, they generally feature a significant degree of flexibility. For instance, community colleges are run by governance boards, whose members can be elected or chosen by the local authorities or by the state. Colleges have the option to adapt training programmes relatively easily, and decisions in this area are taken at local level, rather than state administration level. This enables them to establish customised training programmes designed for employers within a relatively short space of time.
>
> The responsiveness of the education and vocational training system is so great that close links are developed with the local economic fabric. Community colleges are full members of the Workforce Investment Boards (WIBs), institutions responsible for offering

> **Box 5. Examples of flexible education and vocational training systems in Canada (Ontario) and the United States (California and Michigan)** *(cont.)*
>
> employment and training services to individuals in each community (600 throughout the United States), which in turn promotes links with local employers. The partnerships established between community colleges and local businesses have consequently uncovered a number of workforce and skills deficits, and have led to offering training that meets these specific needs.
>
> In the Sacramento region, this collaboration work was promoted by establishing nine centres, whose duties include aligning the training supply with the needs of employers in the region. These centres are situated in 10 areas identified as economic development priority areas. In the State of Michigan, Delta College offers "just-in-time" training over just four weeks. The training is not linked to the academic calendar, and the college calls on external qualified trainers when it does not have the resources to teach certain classes. In the Great Lakes Bay region, personalised training programmes are based on "Fast Start", a partnership between Delta College, the employment agency Michigan Works! Association and employers in key sectors of the local economy. "Fast Start" aims to enable employers who want to create or develop new product lines to have access to a workforce with the requisite skills, both in terms of technical know-how, capacity for working as a team, communication and critical mind-set. Economic development partners first meet with employers so that they can set recruitment criteria as well as the required skills. The duration of the training can range from 12 weeks to 9 months The eligibility prerequisites for the training and the content of the training programmes are decided in collaboration with Delta College. Agencies from the local workforce development network direct their customers towards Delta College, which is responsible for selecting participants for the training. "Fast Start" is designed for individuals able to take part in full-time training, i.e. around 30 hours of class-based training per week, plus between 15 and 20 hours of training outside the college. This accelerated training is primarily suited to candidates who have obtained a university qualification or skills training in a technical field, or for those who have sufficient vocational or military experience.
>
> Source: OECD (2014a), *Employment and Skills Strategies in Canada*, OECD Publishing, Paris, http://dx.doi.org/10.1787/9789264209374-en; OECD (2014b), *Employment and Skills Strategies in the United States*, OECD Reviews on Local Job Creation, OECD Publishing, Paris, http://dx.doi.org/10.1787/9789264209398-en.

1.2. Integration between employment, skills development and economic development

The OECD has demonstrated the importance of de-compartmentalising skills development efforts by co-ordinating them with economic development policies, enabling productivity gains through better use of skills (OECD, 2015a). This was also highlighted at a strategic conference on the skills of the future, organised by the Board of Trade of Metropolitan Montreal in February 2016 (BTMM, 2016). During this conference, which brought together players from industry, education and government, the key role of skills as drivers for boosting productivity and economic prosperity was underlined, as well as the importance of promoting better alignment between these skills and the needs of the business world, since the latter is constantly evolving (BTMM, February 2016).

The multiple measures established by the public authorities in the field of local economic development demonstrate a commitment to supporting the region's economic prosperity. However, in the outcomes of these interventions, there tends to be a lack of co-ordination with local policies on employment and skills. Considerations specific to each organisation, including target customers and priority groups within each of these organisations, tend to take precedence over the collective emergence of an integrated and shared vision of the objectives sought, identifying the expected results, the sharing of resources and appropriate evaluation measures.

Public measures supporting economic development in Montreal are typified by a degree of complexity, with several actors drafting strategies and intervening in connected areas. The federal government is an important player, via Canada Economic Development for Quebec Regions (CED), and the Business Development Bank of Canada (BDC), as are the Port of Montreal (given its responsibilities for bridges) and Pierre-Elliot-Trudeau International Airport. The province of Quebec's Ministry of the Economy, Innovation and Exports (MEIE) also has intervention tools that require a Montreal regional office. The Montreal Metropolitan Community (MMC) has produced a five-year economic development plan, as well as a development and land use plan. Finally, the municipality of Montreal has an economic development office that also produces a strategic development vision.

The Government of Quebec recently undertook a strategy to streamline and pool local and regional economic development resources. In autumn 2014, it abolished the Regional Conference of Elected Representatives (CRE), including that of Montreal, and the programmes of the local development centres (CLDs), whose mandates were devolved to Quebec's municipalities. The municipality of Montreal then reorganised the local development support network by creating, in April 2015, PME MTL, a network of agencies whose role is to encourage the launch and growth of Montreal-based SMEs through a unified service offer that streamlines business processes. Despite these recent rationalisation and streamlining efforts, the institutional framework in local economic development remains complex. For example, the provincial government continues to apply its own planning measures and local development initiatives via its 17 administrative regions.

The emergence of a shared metropolitan vision in Montreal could enable a move towards greater coherence in public policy and improved co-ordination with interventions in the fields of skills development and employment. The Metropolitan Employment Council (CEM) now plays a leading role in this regard, through its mandate to provide knowledge and advice on the labour market situation and key priorities for Montreal's public employment services. The CEM thus advises the five regional offices of *Emploi-Québec* covering the metropolitan area, as well as the central agency and Commission of Labour Market Partners (CPMT), which is the provincial partner agency for employment. Aligning training, skills and employment was identified as one of the two priorities for metropolitan Montreal, the second being the integration of immigrants into the labour market.

The evolution towards "metropolis" status for the municipality of Montreal offers an opportunity to move towards greater integration between economic development, employment and skills development strategies at metropolitan level. The "City Deals" agreed between the British Government and major English cities (see Box 6) and the creation of a new "metropolis" status in France offer interesting lessons on this subject.

1.3. Degree of use of local data for the purposes of formulating policies with measurable results

Use of local data is extensive in Montreal's case, particularly regarding employment and training, where data are more plentiful, more frequent, but also more disaggregated than data on businesses. *Emploi-Québec*'s regional office in Montreal has detailed census data. These

> **Box 6. Examples of devolution of power and responsibilities to major cities that have led to greater integration of local public policies in the United Kingdom and in France**
>
> **The "City Deals" in the United Kingdom**
>
> In the United Kingdom, the "City Deals" are agreements between central government and cities seeking to give local policy makers more powers and freedom, as well as access to new funding mechanisms, in return for a greater degree of responsibility for supporting local economic growth. Skills development is one of the components of the "City Deals". The first wave of agreements was concluded in July 2012 with the eight largest urban areas in the UK outside London. The second wave included 20 cities selected based on their size, as well as their level of demographic growth between 2001 and 2010.
>
> Greater Manchester leads the way in the implementation of these agreements, thanks to strong, stable and effective governance of its metropolitan areas, following the creation of "Greater Manchester Combined Authority" in April 2011. Greater Manchester was able to develop a clear vision of the strengths and weaknesses of its economy, as well as levers that could enable it to realise its development potential. Through the "City Deal", Manchester has:
>
> - Developed a partnership for employment and skills in order to improve knowledge of the local labour market and set priorities and expected results in terms of economic development.
> - Brought together employers, universities and training institutions in order to implement a science academy offering training programmes for young people aged 11 to 18, thus creating a link between the future work force and the region's current strengths in the field of science and technology.
> - Created a city apprenticeship and skills hub able to direct public funds for apprenticeship and skills development towards employers, including SMEs. This gives SMEs more responsibilities within the skills development system, boosting the engagement of employers and private investment in this field.
> - Invested £4 million to encourage SMEs to recruit people seeking jobs, as well as young people not in employment or in training, as apprentices.
>
> **The creation of a new status of "metropole" in France**
>
> In 2014, France introduced a law "empowering metropolises", which created common law metropolises, initially 10, as well as 3 metropolises with special status in Paris, Lyon and Aix-Marseille-Provence. These new forms of inter-communal co-operation exercise full legal powers (in the fields of economic development, planning and housing, for example), in addition to "*à la carte*" powers laid down by local policy makers in each metropolitan area. Metropolises can also sign agreements with other territorial authorities (departmental and regional councils) in order to exercise powers previously attributed to them. This gives them the possibility of playing an increased role in fields such as vocational training, secondary and higher education, and support for innovation.
>
> In this connection, the metropolis of Greater Lyon is a special case, in so far as the 2014 law provides for the transfer of all powers from Rhône departmental council to the metropolis within the latter's area, which includes social and integration policies, as well as support for disadvantaged young people. Greater Lyon has taken up this opportunity to harmonise integration and economic development policies, for which it is now responsible, by establishing a metropolitan employment integration programme (2016-20) following consultation with 250 local partners.

data contain a high number of socio-economic variables, enabling meticulous analysis and identification of specific problems in the Montreal area for each of the 17 CLEs serving individual customers, and for the two centres that specialise in services for businesses. Other information sources are also available to local authorities, and they are routinely exploited in analytical exercises and when formulating policies and their resultant directions.

For example, *Emploi-Québec*'s regional office in Montreal is conducting a survey into training and workforce needs at establishments on the Island of Montreal with five or more employees. The study covers themes such as number of appointments during the past 12 months, recruitment problems, training needs, planned appointments during the next 12 months, and immigration and human resources. However, the latest survey dates back to 2012. These data are incredibly useful in the decisions of officials and customers regarding training and job seeking, and they enable business advisers to identify more clearly the businesses, sectors and issues for which support from public services can make a real difference.

There is also a great deal of in-depth administrative data concerning customers. Data on participation and the results of this participation are evaluated, leading, where applicable, to adjustments in approach or in the targeting of customers. In addition, *Emploi-Québec* obtains data from the Online Placement website or from the LMI website about the characteristics of the businesses and individuals using them. A directory of businesses in the area is also kept up to date, through a joint effort by ministries and public bodies, and this directory is accessible to job seekers and CLE staff.

The data available on SMEs are, however, primarily from databases that are not systematically updated by statistics agencies, as are the employment and labour market data. This is due in large part to the difficulty of monitoring a population – that of SMEs – that is constantly changing due to a high rate of business start-ups and failures, and to changes in status and size. For their part, official statistics agencies have limited programs for the analysis of metropolitan data. In so far as they exist and are reliable, local data are therefore routinely used and exploited. This is true for federal, provincial, regional and municipal bodies.

Partnership, dialogue, consultation and collaboration between different actors in joint agencies such as the CEM are favoured approaches to understanding needs, alongside statistical data. The mission of the CEM is wide-ranging, as is its composition. It brings together leading institutional policy makers such as the Board of Trade of Metropolitan Montreal, as well as the South Shore Board of Trade; *Montréal International*, whose mission is to attract foreign investment, foreign workers and international organisations to Montreal; the aerospace and digital technology clusters; a university representative and another from the CEGEP grouping in the area; the metropolitan regional councils of the two major groups of affiliated trade unions; the MMC; and the municipality of Montreal's Economic Development Department. This membership ensures that there is strong representation of metropolitan actors, a high quality of analysis and opinion, and careful consideration by political and administrative authorities.

The challenge of obtaining quality local data that are relevant and up to date was also identified by the Final Report of the Advisory Panel on Labour Market Information in Canada (2009). In particular, the panel suggested that Statistics Canada should expand and invest heavily in this area. The budgetary and policy direction of the previous federal government led to significant reductions in funds and to the disappearance or (temporary) reduction of the scope of certain surveys, but this situation has been corrected by the Trudeau Government. Continued, broader investment in surveys and information at all levels is strongly recommended for Montreal.

The issue of local data was also highlighted as part of the "*Je vois Montréal*" and "*Je fais Montréal*" project (see Box 17). A local development indicator is currently being prepared to gain a clearer understanding of all dimensions of local development beyond economic growth.

Theme 2: Creation of a productive local economy – adding value through skills and avoiding the low skills equilibrium trap

The second chapter of this report highlighted Montreal's deficit in the supply and demand of skills, which is reflected in a low level of productivity in workers in comparison with other OECD metropolises. This theme aims to assess the strengths and weaknesses of local public policies in supporting the creation of a productive local economy through training the workforce, engaging employers in the formulation of skills development policies, and providing support for SMEs.

Figure 3.3. **Creation of a productive economy through skills**

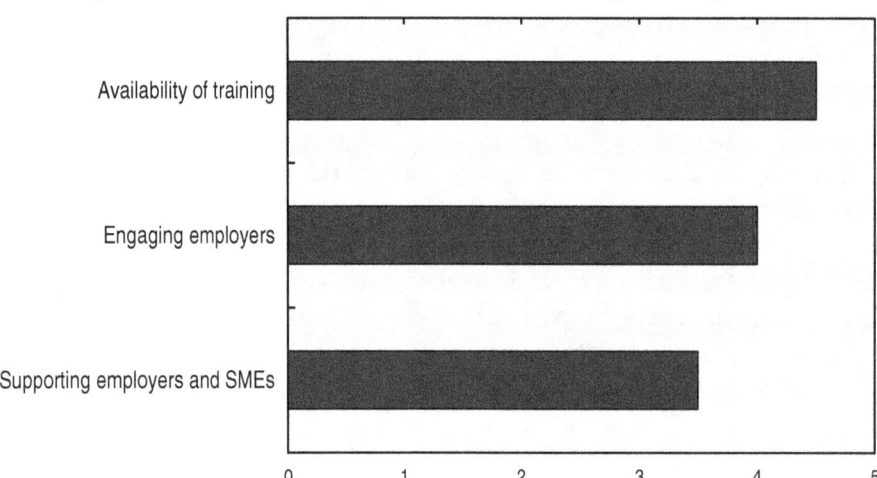

2.1. A broad training offer open to all

A wide range of training courses is available in Montreal. *Emploi-Québec* offers unemployed people wishing to enter the job market the opportunity to undertake, subject to certain conditions, full-time training in a variety of fields of study. Over 75 programmes were available in 2015-16. These training courses are selected based on a needs analysis of the labour market in Montreal, as a supplement to the regular supply from educational institutions accessible to all interested persons. This training primarily leads to STC and ACS-type awards following sessions varying between 300 and 1 500 hours. It is primarily school boards, via their network of secondary schools, and the CEGEPs of the Island of Montreal that are called on to deliver this training. An annual directory of training financed by *Emploi-Québec* is available online for further information.

As a large city with an education and training infrastructure that is highly developed at all levels of education (more than 200 secondary-level schools, within the remit of the

Island's four school boards, 12 CEGEPs and four universities, in addition to private general, vocational and technical training institutions) and a large pool of individuals undertaking training or wishing to undertake training or perfect their skills, Montreal enjoys an undeniable advantage in this field compared with other less densely populated areas outside Quebec or Canada.

Subsidised training for unemployed people and workers, basic training, literacy, francisation, English as a second language, modular training and after-work training are widely available. Financial aid from *Emploi-Québec* can also be offered under certain conditions. Occasionally, certain training courses cannot go ahead, due to low enrolment numbers. The training calendar and timescales before the start of a training course can also create barriers to entry. Finally, financial constraints prevent some people who are not eligible for support from federal or provincial income from having access to full-time training. Montreal is not alone in this, as has been shown by various studies, including studies by the Mowat Centre (2013), which advocates a pan-Canadian measure offering loans and bursaries to adults for vocational training in order to plug the gaps in this area.

2.2. Employers' role and involvement in skills development

The capacity of training to meet the needs of employers has been a subject of debate in Montreal for several years. Various aspects come into play, such as knowing whether the public training system can and should accommodate the often specific, one-off requests expressed by individual employers or whether, by contrast, they should aim for vocational training that meets the present *and* future needs of all labour market players. Vocational training that is more holistic helps to balance the supply and demand of skills at local level, facilitates people's mobility between jobs and enables them to move to more productive and therefore better paid jobs. Such mobility does not necessarily meet the needs of each individual employer, but it improves the general functioning of the labour market, productivity and, consequently, workers' remuneration.

Progress can and should be made in aligning training to the needs of the labour market, but there is no consensus on how this should happen, nor on an unequivocal indicator of success. However, several initiatives are moving in this direction, such as the roll-out of dedicated vocational or technical schools. In its speech on the 2015-2016 budget, the Government of Quebec announced new measures and further increased resources in order to improve the alignment between training and employment, for example by extending the apprenticeship scheme and its associated tax credits.

Although studies and surveys on the issue of the training drive financed by employers are not as enlightening as one might hope, various surveys with a range of methodologies have repeatedly cited low levels of contribution from employers over the years.[1] It is clear that the law instructing businesses with a total wage bill of CAD 2 million or more to allocate at least 1% of this to expenditure on recognised training has not changed the situation significantly. A number of factors have been put forward to explain this, such as the large proportion of SMEs in the Montreal area, the industry mix more focused towards traditional industries, workers' lower level of schooling, and low private investment in machinery and equipment, which often in turn triggers a need for investment in training. The partial data available show that contributions by SMEs sit at a level below 0.5% of the total wage bill (at least the contribution to structured and measurable training), and over 1% in large businesses. In the case of the latter, the contribution can be significantly higher in certain strongly competitive and globalised high value-added sectors.

Public support is granted to employers' associations and to large businesses that agree to support skills development within SMEs. Thus, the Commission of Labour Market Partners (CPMT) finances the activities of 29 sectoral committees whose role is to identify the development needs of the workforce in their particular industry and to support skills development using tools such as skills standards and apprenticeship schemes. The CPMT, which counts major employers' associations as members, also encourages training through the *Investissement-compétences* (Skills Investment) initiative, which seeks to mobilise and encourage businesses and workers to establish a coherent strategy of investing in the skills of the workforce, and to promote a continuous training culture in workplaces.

Large businesses in highly integrated, high-tech sectors such as aerospace encourage and even require their suppliers and subcontractors to invest in training. The aim of the continuous training of workers, chiefly the least qualified, is not, however, reflected in any obvious way in the practice of all businesses. Specific programmes and initiatives are nevertheless established in order to increase training in the workplace. Thus, the *Emploi-Québec* regional office in Montreal provides services to over 2 300 businesses annually. There are, however, over 100 000 businesses in the metropolitan area, the large majority being SMEs. The training supported by the regional office can take different forms, including training in the workplace or at a training institution, or the mixed approach offered by apprenticeship.

> #### Box 7. **Aerospace training**
>
> The Montreal metropolitan area is the third largest in the world in terms of the number of workers in the aerospace industry, after Seattle and Toulouse. Over the years, leading-edge guidance institutions, such as the Quebec Sectoral Aerospace Workforce Committee (CAMAQ), responsible for identifying the industry's needs in staff and skills, providing recommendations to training authorities and supporting businesses through the development of skills management and development tools for their personnel, have emerged in the metropolitan region. The *Aéro Montréal* Montreal-based cluster, meanwhile, brings together key businesses and business leaders with a strategic focus of growing the industry.
>
> The Montreal aerospace industry also has two public teaching establishments dedicated to it: the Montreal Aerospace Trade School (EMAM), which offers a wide range of post-secondary vocational training programmes, and the National Institute of Aeronautics (ENA), which offers vocational training in several specialisations. Finally, Montreal's universities also offer engineering programmes focused on the aerospace industry.
>
> The programmes are designed and developed in close collaboration with industry, which also supports the schools, for example by providing them with state-of-the-art training equipment.

For their part, school boards, CEGEPs and universities put graduates and local employers in contact with each other, for example through placement services at schools or job fairs. These contributions are particularly important where training is directly linked to locally dominant economic sectors in Montreal, such as ICT, aeronautics, engineering, film and television, and finance.

In addition to these targeted contributions by teaching institutions to matching the supply and demand of skills, *Emploi-Québec* operates a placement and labour market information service, *IMT en ligne*. Around 550 000 vacancies, itemised by profession and region, are posted each year. The Canadian Government, meanwhile, operates an online job bank (*Guichet Emploi*), which advertises over 100 000 vacancies on average at any time across Canada. Although all occupations can be posted on these sites, the majority of posts are for positions with average or low levels of qualifications. More highly qualified positions are generally recruited through other channels. Employers who hire highly qualified workers often use their own company website or specialist private websites. In the case of Montreal, highly detailed information on the posts available by municipal district and by profession can be accessed. Around 150 000 vacancies are posted each year for the Montreal area on the Online Placement website. It should nevertheless be noted that public-sector institutions such as the CEGEPs and health-care institutions do not post their vacancies on this site. However, these areas of health and education alone employ more than 10% of Montreal's workers.

2.3. Use of skills, organisation of work, human resources management: support for Montreal's SMEs

Two specialist centres of *Emploi-Québec*'s regional office in Montreal aim to support and encourage better use of skills by employers in various ways. The *Task Forces on Employment* scheme offers various aids including:

- Business diagnosis regarding human resources;
- Management assistance (coaching);
- The establishment of a task force within the business, so that it can adapt to major changes that could jeopardise jobs. This task force analyses problems, proposes solutions and oversees the implementation of an action plan and its follow-up;
- Support for human resources management by a specialist in order to, for example, improve recruitment practices, skills development, job retention and performance appraisals;
- The establishment of a human resources department.

The skills development drive therefore goes beyond training alone, to encompass all of the issues relating to development and to the full use of skills. Human resources dedicated to these tasks are, however, limited, and use of specialist external resources for the provision of services is widespread.

The Montreal regional office of the Ministry of the Economy, Science and Innovation (MESI) also offers advice and tools to employers on human resource management. Support for public services is primarily intended for small businesses. Programmes can be adapted to individual contexts, and a network of representatives (intermediaries) helps to engage SMEs in skills and knowledge development. This network includes workforce sectoral committees, training mutuals, as well as an extensive network of private consultants, many of whom are paid through government support offered to SMEs.

The sector-based approach is fairly extensive in Montreal, where the majority of Quebec's 29 sectoral committees operate. They do, however, have varying impact on the businesses and workers targeted. They aim to establish skills profiles, to estimate workforce and training needs and to provide tools to employers. In general, the sectoral committees have a more limited impact on the populations targeted by their initiatives in more traditional sectors, which typically have a large number of small businesses and workers with lower levels of qualification. Box 8 shows the factors involved in a successful sectoral initiative in the catering industry in Boston (United States). In Flanders, "experimental laboratories" have enabled innovative work organisations to be implemented in a range of different sectors (Box 9).

> ### Box 8. Example of an initiative promoting the development and use of employees' skills in Boston, United States
>
> Over the past decade, sectoral initiatives and strategies to support occupational mobility have dominated policies in the field of skills development in the United States. Sectoral initiatives are based on the idea that, in order to reduce the gap between supply and demand of skills, and to provide more opportunities for workers with little job security, the latter must be trained in high-demand trades that are well paid and that offer opportunities for career advancement. These initiatives benefit both employees and employers, the latter benefiting from productivity gains and lower staff turnover.
>
> The catering industry is one of the sectors experiencing the highest growth in the United States. While it accounts for over 8% of total employment, this industry features a particularly high proportion of workers at or below the minimum wage (around 39% of the workforce). Individuals with jobs associated with the preparation of food and with service received a median hourly wage of USD 9.02 (including tips) in 2010, which is below the poverty line for a full-time worker whose household has two children.
>
> Paris Creperie, situated in Brookline, Greater Boston (Massachusetts), is a café and restaurant selling products including authentic traditional French crêpes in an environment typical of European cafés. The establishment also has a mobile restaurant, an online booking platform and a catering service for business customers or for events in the city of Boston. Paris Creperie recently set up, with the support of consulting firm Delta Foodservices, an open-book management ("Open Book Solutions") method, intended for all of its employees. This method involves training staff in the principles of accounting and management by teaching them aspects such as how to interpret the company's accounting and financial statements. Employees' aptitude for solving problems and entrepreneurial skills are also developed. Finally, employees are given the opportunity to take initiatives to reduce costs and propose new business opportunities, thus ensuring productivity as well as a lower rate of staff turnover thanks to greater employee involvement. The training modules have been designed to be mutually reinforcing and include case studies to promote learning processes and practical application to the realities of work at Paris Creperie. This new organisation within the business has enabled employees to develop their skills in different areas: implementation and monitoring of a staff budget; improving personal knowledge in finance (including the ability to understand and interpret the company's financial data and accounting records); measuring progress; problem-solving, which includes identifying challenges and opportunities for the business; and taking the initiative to seize new business opportunities and reduce inefficiencies. Finally, a leadership training module was implemented in order to strengthen capacities for the management of staff, skills and performance.
>
> One year after the establishment of this new form of organisation of work, the project was considered a great success by all staff. Having overcome initial scepticism, practical results were achieved in terms of increased profitability, better pay for employees through the payment of substantial bonuses, and reduced staff turnover.
>
> Source: OECD (forthcoming, 2016), *Moving Employers to More Productive Jobs*, OECD Publishing, Paris.

> **Box 9. Testing innovative ways of organising work through "experimental laboratories" in Flanders**
>
> In Limburg, the "experimental laboratories for innovative ways of organising work" were set up with employers as part of a broader programme to provide solutions to problems associated with demographic change and an ageing population. The trade union ACV played an important role in the development and practical implementation of this initiative. Initially set up in different industries (construction, logistics, health, the social economy, social services and agriculture, for example), the experimental laboratories were freed from sectoral constraints in order to favour a thematic approach and foster discussion exchanges between a wider range of firms. The laboratories can accommodate SMEs and large companies alike.
>
> In 2014, eight workshops, each involving between six and eight companies, were held. A consultant was asked to work on running the workshops, which operated as knowledge-sharing networks between businesses. Business executives were encouraged to think about ways of changing management practices in order to ensure greater employee involvement in the company's various activities. Each laboratory covers seven themes corresponding to different aspects that may be subject to changes in the organisation of work. For example, one of the themes related to ways in which companies can invest in new markets in order to improve organisational performance as well as job quality. Practical exercises were also provided so that participants could translate theory into practical changes within their organisation.
>
> Source: OECD (2015b), "Employment and Skills Strategies in Flanders, Belgium", *OECD Reviews on Local Job Creation*, OECD Publishing, Paris, http://dx.doi.org/10.1787/9789264228740-en.

Theme 3. Supporting entrepreneurship, innovation and economic development

Figure 3.4. **Entrepreneurship, economic development and innovation**

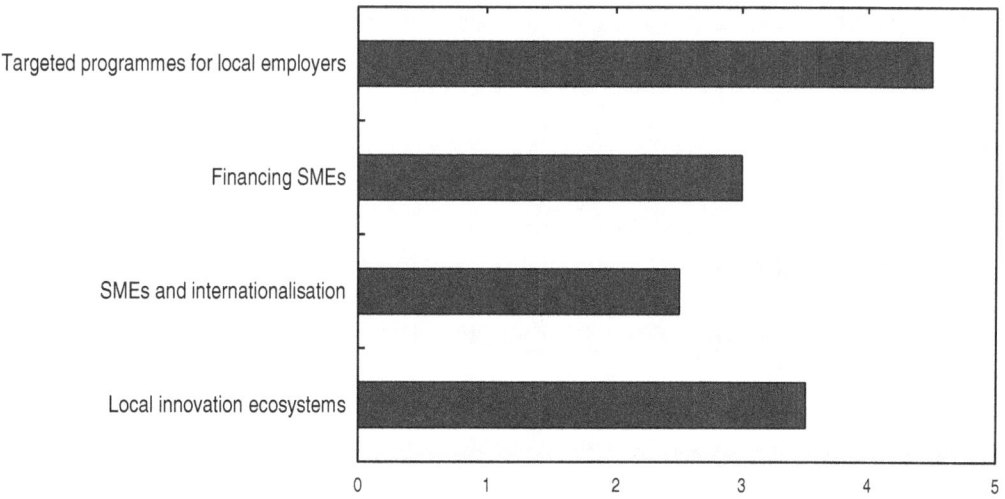

3.1. Meeting the specific needs of SMEs by adapting programmes and services

Although most programmes supporting local development and the bulk of their budgets come from the provincial and federal governments, the municipality of Montreal also devises and administers some of them. The municipality spends approximately

CAD 100 million per year on economic development programmes, i.e. approximately 2% of its total budget. Although they are not routinely targeted at SMEs, programmes and fiscal measures from all three levels of government are often reserved for SMEs.

Following the abolition by the Quebec Government of the local development centres in autumn 2014, the municipality of Montreal has reorganised the model of public support for local economic development. In April 2015, it created PME MTL, a network of non-profit organisations across the Island of Montreal area whose role is to support the launch and growth of Montreal-based SMEs. PME MTL offers a range of professional services, such as advice on management and funding decisions, which are available to private business and social economy leaders, and it works in collaboration with a network of partners. The majority of services offered by the PME MTL network are free of charge.

The municipality of Montreal has also launched the *Parcours Innovation PME Montréal* (Montreal SME Innovation Course) initiative. Supported by the Government of Quebec and receiving support from several private and public partners, this pilot project aims to offer SMEs located on the Island of Montreal a structured assistance approach to stimulate their growth and gain a foothold in international markets. The municipality's modest resources available in this field, however, limit the scope of the initiative. Consequently, only 30 SMEs per year have been able to benefit from this pilot project to date.

Courses on business skills are provided at educational and training institutions at various levels. These courses are primarily set up on an *ad hoc* basis in secondary schools. CEGEPs and universities also offer these courses, although knowledge and take-up of these courses are not very widespread. Coaching of SMEs by large companies is rare, except in certain industries where industrial structures are favourable, i.e. where a few large companies are acting as leaders and principals, and are therefore seeking long-term business partners.

3.2. Facilitating access to financing for SMEs

Montreal is a leading financial centre. It is home to major institutions, including the main Canadian banks, the Quebec Deposit and Investment Fund, *Investissement Québec*, the *Fonds de Solidarité FTQ* and the Business Development Bank of Canada. Venture capital remains a component where needs are yet to be met. Small businesses that have been operating for a few years and want to grow often have an urgent need for capital where there is no expectation of immediate returns, a willingness to take on significant risks, as well as the possibility of offering supervised support to the leaders of these businesses. In recent years, a significant number of new firms specialising in venture capital have emerged, particularly in the information and communication technology (ICT) and clean/green technologies sectors.

Venture capital provides financial support, but it can also, depending on the degree of maturity of the industry, provide support for young entrepreneurs whose ideas merit expert support in areas where the entrepreneur has shortcomings, needs advice or mentoring or would benefit from sharing experiences, whether in human resources, marketing, legal or regulatory knowledge, insurance or other matters directly related to the business itself.

Government aid and publicly-funded programmes for SMEs in the start-up phase, and even more so at pre-start-up phase, including subsidies and credit guarantees, are limited in scope and are not easily accessible, even though they appear not to be in short supply. This situation of low financing is unlikely to change in the short term given the public finance objectives pursued at provincial and federal level. At municipal level, the resources available fall far short of ambitions, and the legal constraints arising from the various provincial laws severely limit the support that Montreal can offer to businesses. Although PME MTL offers financing solutions for certain SMEs, mainly in the form of grants and loans, the amounts allocated so far remain relatively modest. The advisory and support role of PME MTL regarding access to financing should nevertheless be stressed, particularly in view of the complexity of public and private financing channels and the multiple funds available (local investment fund, local development capital fund, business start-ups funds, etc.). Furthermore, an agreement was recently signed between PME MTL and the Desjardins Group in order to improve financing for entrepreneurs aged between 18 and 35 in the process of starting a business on the Island of Montreal.

Tax expenditures are a less visible aspect of government aid to businesses, including SMEs. Tax expenditures are where a government agrees to forego revenue by implementing fiscal mechanisms, mainly tax credits, which allow eligible businesses to reduce their taxable income or allow for offsetting certain eligible expenses. These mechanisms have increased over the years but without our knowing precisely whether they meet the objectives set. There are around 90 in Quebec, according to the 2014 report of the Quebec Taxation Review Committee. Their value clearly exceeds the programmes' expenditure. Montreal-based businesses particularly benefit from such federal or provincial mechanisms, whose intention is to promote research, development, innovation and exports, or to stimulate an industry considered strategic.

For example, there are tax credits for wages in the multimedia industries, the International Financial Centre and the Montreal Foreign Trade Zone at Mirabel, as well as for research and development activities. These tax credits also proportionally benefit Montreal-based businesses, as the industries and activities targeted are highly concentrated in Montreal. It appears that the performance of these intervention tools needs to be reviewed more closely, and that choices could be made as a result of such a review to target aid and expectations more accurately and to focus resources on a limited number of sectors or objectives.

Box 10. **Provincial laws restricting Montreal action regarding aid to businesses**

A series of provincial laws govern and limit action by Montreal and other Quebec municipalities, particularly in the area of providing aid to local businesses. These laws have in common that they prohibit the municipality from subsidising a business, with a few rare exceptions. However, Montreal has interesting opportunities regarding municipal contracts, experimental projects – for example in testing vacant or underutilised land decontamination technology, crucial for the development of certain industrial wastelands – and the use of disused urban buildings that could serve as incubators for new businesses. These are just some examples of initiatives that Montreal wants to be able to implement. Ongoing discussions with the Quebec Government on metropolis status address these questions. Rather than having to meet, *a priori*, multiple requirements and comply with guidelines from several provincial government departments and bodies, Montreal is seeking a *modus operandi* in which transparency of procedures and accountability constitute, *a posteriori*, the new reality of relations with the provincial government, the municipal government and the citizens of Montreal.

3.3. Supporting SMEs in their international development

The main obstacles facing businesses in this area are the high costs of internationalisation, the lack of information on foreign market opportunities, and laws and regulations governing these markets. The current weakness of the Canadian dollar has recently been a favourable factor, but it does not create sufficient conditions for the internationalisation of Montreal-based SMEs, let alone long-term certainty.

A number of aid mechanisms exist to promote the international expansion of Quebec's SMEs. For example, one of the objectives of *Parcours Innovation PME Montréal* is to encourage SMEs to develop strategies for expansion into international markets.

However, it seems that they are not running at their full potential, mainly due to lack of awareness of the programmes and the organisations that manage them. The organisations most utilised by SMEs are Export Development Canada (EDC), Quebec's Ministry of the Economy, Innovation and Exports (MEIE), the BDC, the Community Futures Development Corporations (CFDCs) and Industry Canada, in that order. Leaders with university education use these various programmes the most. Some organisations are practically unknown to SMEs (Majlinda and Niosi, 2011). By contrast, many businesses make use of the R&D tax credits. However, SMEs that engage in research and development are much more likely than others to be export businesses. Measures supporting the internationalisation of businesses should be as widespread as possible, and be part of all programmes. Officials assigned to implementing the various programmes should better understand the other support organisations in order to direct businesses towards the programmes that best suit their needs when they meet with SME business leaders. In addition, organisations must stress the need to innovate and develop quality control programmes, two important factors in internationalisation.

> **Box 11. The business permit and licensing portal (BizPal)**
>
> A frequent recrimination of SMEs in Montreal has to do with difficulties in accessing information on obligations, and on the various aids available. Navigating the various administrations to obtain this information is a long and costly process. The BizPal portal is an innovative response where all three levels of government pool information in a virtual one-stop shop.
>
> This research tool lists the permits and licenses required to operate a business in the central district of Montreal. These permits are issued by one of the three levels of government: municipal, provincial and federal. The 18 other districts of Montreal (other than the central district of Ville-Marie) have not yet submitted information about them on this site.
>
> The BizPal portal is localised on the *Services Québec* website, which also provides detailed information on aid programmes, federal and provincial laws and regulations, as well as on support for businesses available from various non-governmental organisations. However, there is no information concerning the municipal administration, which creates a void that must be filled so that all business people have access to all relevant and useful information regarding aid and programmes.

Several factors may explain the lack of support for internationalisation aimed at SMEs in the area, despite recognition of the importance of this objective for the growth of these businesses and for the prosperity of the Quebec and Montreal economy. Beyond budgetary constraints common to other areas, there are practical difficulties relating to the mobilisation of small businesses. The problem of the parcelling out and dispersal of aid among multiple agencies and programmes, many of which have modest resources, creates an obstacle to the full use of existing aid. Although the BizPal virtual one-stop shop is an undeniable step forward, it does not replace a physical one-stop service or personalised assistance. Rather, it is a complement to these. BizPal does not resolve the problem of the proliferation, parcelling out and dispersal of measures and resources.

Support for the internationalisation of SMEs may require presence at international trade shows, or organising more personalised business meetings (business to business, B2B). The "matching" initiative in Italy is an interesting example of connecting businesses that may encourage the formation of business networks at local and international level (Box 12).

> ### Box 12. **Customised, effective business meetings in Italy**
>
> "Matching" is an innovative business-to-business (B2B) initiative which is organised annually by the Compagnia delle Opere (CDO), an Italian entrepreneurial association with over 34 000 corporate members, mostly small firms, and supported by the Ministry of Economic Development, the National Association of Chambers of Commerce and the Lombardy regional government. Its main purpose is to foster the creation of networks of firms, with particular emphasis on the utilisation of network contracts and collaboration between SMEs and large firms.
>
> The cornerstone of "Matching" is a national three-day event held in Milan every year involving on average over 2 000 firms, institutions and supporting bodies, and generating over 50 000 B2B appointments. During this national event, over 100 thematic workshops take place, supported by a network of experts in a variety of fields (exporting, innovation, etc.). The event has two critical success factors. First, there is on an online matching mechanism which allows participants to develop an agenda of pre-matched B2B appointments before the event. Local CDO advisers regularly incentivise firms to prepare their online virtual showrooms, scan the list of other participants and send appointment requests. Second, all local advisers regularly check each participant's list of appointments to increase the effectiveness of the event and to offer suggestions for additional synergies. An analysis of the 2011 edition suggests that firms conducted an average of 41 business meetings during the three days, out of which 11 were judged as useful and 4 led very quickly to new commercial or partnership exchanges.
>
> The national event is complemented by events organised by the 40 CDO local branches. These local events typically involve between 150 and 300 participants and aim to facilitate continuous interactions among participants during the year. Building on a network of foreign branches in 17 countries, the CDO has also started to organise mini-"Matching" events based on the same formula in countries such as Brazil, China, Qatar, Russia and Spain, with the objective of supporting the internationalisation of its SME members.
>
> Source: OECD (2014c), "National programmes for SMEs and entrepreneurship in Italy", in OECD, Italy: Key Issues and Policies, OECD Publishing, Paris, http://dx.doi.org/10.1787/9789264213951-9-en.

3.4. Encouraging the sharing of knowledge through the development of local entrepreneurship and innovation ecosystems

The meso-economic dimension, the intermediary between the main macro-economic aggregates and individual and business data, has gained in importance from a theoretical and analytical perspective in recent years via the innovation system concept (Nelson, 2000). This dimension refers to the institutional, social, urban, cultural, fiscal and political context, which is considered an explanatory factor for the situations observed in the economic theory of innovation. It is also interesting to note that the innovation system concept is frequently discussed at regional or even metropolitan level in a number of studies and publications, because notions of proximity and density are fundamental in this approach (Cooke, 2001).

Studies on entrepreneurship and innovation emphasise the importance of local ecosystems and assistance networks, knowledge sharing and co-innovation. In the current context, innovation is becoming increasingly open and transverse in different fields and institutions of human activity (Cohendet et al., 2009). The notion of intellectual property is gradually changing, since the free and spontaneous sharing of ideas is increasingly becoming a guarantee of success for those who practice it.

Moreover, agglomeration economies give dense urban areas a crucial advantage in terms of productivity and innovation by promoting the transmission of knowledge, the pooling of resources and the matching of supply and demand on the markets for goods, services and labour (Puga, 2010). As a metropolitan area with over 4 million inhabitants, Montreal has a critical mass that allows substantial agglomeration economies in several areas: industrial structures, supply, immediate market opportunities, labour market, universities and colleges, highly qualified workers, immigrants and research institutions. But it is often argued that such a critical mass concentrated in a relatively small area is an essential ingredient of a successful innovation ecosystem (Knudsen et al., 2008).

Networking and interaction processes between innovators are present in Montreal, particularly among young entrepreneurs working in information and communication technology. There are venues, tools and events that promote spontaneous and exploratory discussions (see Boxes 13 and 14). Unfortunately, the existence of some venues is often precarious, because they depend on changing public policies that are not sufficiently aligned with a long-term strategy. Per-project financing also requires them to comply with standards or mandatory guidelines, and to engage in punishing and almost continuous operational fund-raising exercises.

> ### Box 13. **Technical Arts Society (TAS)**
>
> Founded in 1996, the Technical Arts Society (TAS) is a non-profit organisation known for its active and pioneering role in the development of immersive technologies (augmented reality through the creative use of superfast broadband networks). With its dual mission as an arts and research centre, the TAS was created to support a new generation of designers/researchers in the digital era.
>
> Located on Saint Laurent Boulevard in Montreal, the southern gate of the arts and entertainment district (*Quartier des Spectacles*), the TAS has become a vital meeting space and a place where everything is possible, where "positive contamination" between the arts, science and technology sectors makes the TAS an innovation partner at the crossroads of these three key economic pillars.
>
> Simultaneously an engine and a showcase of IT innovations applied to art and design, the TAS is an important indicator of their social and economic significance. It brings together research, training, design and distribution under one roof. This organisational model has earned the TAS an invitation as the first North American member of the Open Living Labs network ENoLL, a European initiative bringing together over 200 research and innovation centres worldwide.

> **Box 14. Montreal International Start-up Festival (Startupfest)**
>
> This annual event, created in 2011, aims to be unforgettable and unconventional. It focuses on entrepreneurship and start-ups, and attracts people from many different countries.
>
> The Festival includes a "conventional" component: talks, interactive sessions, training and networking. The various aspects and stages of starting a business are addressed by young entrepreneurs with whom participants can easily identify and who are likely to provide them with practical advice on launching and managing their projects.
>
> There is also a host of related activities likely to promote the development of ideas, building bridges, establishing alliances. The Festival is held in July, and participants can also benefit from the many events that bring the city to life during this time of year.
>
> The decidedly international focus of the Festival is very important because it broadens the horizons of aspiring entrepreneurs and introduces them to people whose experiences offer a wealth of information and with whom these aspiring entrepreneurs can establish long-lasting, broader networks.

The desire to become an entrepreneur appears low overall in Quebec, in comparison with other regions of Canada (BDC, June 2010). The challenges around growing a business can also become a burden for many entrepreneurs, who prefer to divest themselves of their business once it reaches a threshold that requires a complex managerial structure, listing on the stock market, external venture capital, mergers, acquisitions or an export strategy – all things that could require more innovation and productivity gains, but which also profoundly change the daily life of the entrepreneur.

Several institutions and intermediaries in Montreal aim to encourage entrepreneurship and to support businesses at different stages of their growth (see Box 15). Incubators host fledgling projects that were made possible thanks to seed money, which usually comes from public programmes. Accelerators aim for rapid propulsion of promising small businesses. Venture capital often features at this stage or further on, when the business is well positioned to become a significant player in its field, even internationally. It is important to maintain and expand these assistance institutions and the expertise they offer.

Public authorities are still ill-adapted to supporting new innovation processes and instead prioritise initiatives that fit with a traditional sector-based model of public intervention aimed primarily at assisting an individual or a sole proprietorship. The innovation policy implemented by the Government of Quebec adopts this approach. The Government of Quebec has opted not to adopt an overall research and innovation strategy, preferring to offer businesses financial products for their investment projects individually, as part of the "*Créativité Québec*" programme launched in 2014, and with a budget of CAD 150 million over three years. Moreover, the existing committees and working groups are still not producing results that measure up to expectations regarding collaboration between universities, colleges, industry and government. Expectations of short-term tangible results that frequently guide public intervention do not sit well with the approach of interpenetration of expertise and diverse fields, the benefits of which require a maturation time that often exceeds the investment horizon of governments. Nurturing innovation requires patience and guidance based on trust, and must be consistent over time. However, recurring shifts in focus and frequent reorganisations of public measures are not in step with these innovation contexts.

> **Box 15. Examples of organisations involved in supporting entrepreneurship and business development**
>
> **Fondation Montréal Inc.**
>
> *Fondation Montréal Inc.* is a non-profit organisation with a mission to encourage the success of a new generation of promising Montreal entrepreneurs, in consultation with a committed business community. Thanks to the generosity of its donors and volunteers – experienced business people – the foundation is able to invest in newly created businesses in Montreal through start-up grants and expert advice. Networking between new entrepreneurs is also fostered through various activities that can be formal or informal in nature. The foundation is an organisation supported by the Montreal business community and all three levels of government. The Mayor of Montreal serves on its board of directors.
>
> The foundation invests in the creation, expansion and continued support of promising businesses to help build the Montreal of tomorrow. Since its creation in 1996, the foundation has awarded over CAD 6.7 million in grants to help to help 853 start-up businesses in Montreal, which have in turn generated over 2 754 jobs. The foundation has thus contributed to creating over CAD 61 million in investments in Montreal.
>
> **Centre d'Entreprises et d'Innovation de Montréal**
>
> The *Centre d'Entreprises et d'Innovation de Montréal* (Montreal Business and Innovation Centre – CEIM) provides customised management and consulting and related services for start-up companies in information technology, new media, clean and industrial technologies; start-up companies in life sciences; the expansion of information technology businesses (marketing support) and the development of life science businesses.
>
> CEIM aims to identify business projects with strong commercial and growth potential; offer a range of specialised, efficient and affordable services that respond to the specific needs of these projects; increase business survival and success probabilities; and enhance entrepreneurship and Quebec's economic development.
>
> **Examples of incubators: Notman House and XPND Capital**
>
> A historic building that has been used for various purposes since its construction in 1844, **Notman House** has been leased since 2011 by the firm Real Ventures, a venture capital company that provides not only funds but also ongoing support and advice for the benefit of its project partners. Real Ventures has made Notman House a new technology business incubator. Notman House has 23 private offices for rent for the high-tech start-up community. By having an office at Notman House, each day new entrepreneurs are immersed in an environment designed to support entrepreneurs backed by Real Ventures, working with a community of people in similar situations who can share their experiences, questions and ideas.
>
> **XPND Capital** aims to help build the next generation of large successful companies in Quebec by bringing strategic capital and expertise and collaborating with entrepreneurs in their growth phase. The firm seeks to partner with established businesses with strong potential for growth and profitability operating in its target industries, following a thorough due diligence process. Together with the businesses in which XPNP invests, it develops and participates in the implementation of a business strategy to accelerate growth and maximise market share in order to realise full revenue and profit potential. XPND also acts as a platform, promoting merger, acquisition and integration to the benefit of companies with potential to consolidate their market.

The municipality of Montreal, meanwhile, has modest means for supporting local development, innovation and entrepreneurship processes. While the preferred approach has long been primarily sectoral, through support for industrial clusters, the municipality's culture in this field is nevertheless gradually evolving. The Mayor of Montreal has shown a willingness to play a facilitating role in this area by creating an environment conducive to creativity and business (Ville de Montréal, 21 January 2016). At his impetus, the municipality decided to support projects such as the *Quartier de l'Innovation* (Innovation District, see Box 16), but also initiatives as part of a "bottom up" approach to economic development, similar to "*Je vois/Je fais Montréal*" (see Box 17). It has also chosen to focus on entrepreneurs and SMEs by offering individualised support solutions to certain businesses, in particular through *Parcours Innovation PME Montréal* and PME MTL, albeit with relatively limited resources.

Box 16. Montreal Quartier de l'Innovation

In the 20th century, largely due to the advent of the motor car, cities expanded by spatially separating urban functions: some districts were exclusively designed for residential use, others industrial or commercial, and others institutional or recreational. The consequence of this mode of development was the promotion of urban sprawl and low density, increasing travel and minimising interactions between people moving around in different areas, and therefore physically distant from each other. Many cities are now looking to move away from this model by increasing the density of occupation of the territory and by focusing this on the mixed nature and verticality of functions that were previously separate, for example by concentrating commercial activities on the ground floor of buildings that house offices and have housing on the upper floors.

Located in a former industrial area near the city centre, whose regeneration began largely following the establishment of the *École de Technologie Supérieure* (ETS) engineering faculty, the *Quartier de l'Innovation* (QI) is first and foremost a project for the integration and interconnection of the four essential components of a creative society that make up an innovation ecosystem of global proportions in Montreal:

The urban component concerns sustainable development, services for the municipality and citizens, green spaces, respect for history and heritage, public transport and shared infrastructure management. For many stakeholders in the innovation field, the need for greater investment in physical and virtual environments, places and events promoting the exchange of ideas and knowledge is a priority still poorly understood by public authorities, which favour more traditional, consulting-type instruments, training and grants to a single business rather than to networking schemes.

The training and research component: the training of the next generation of highly qualified staff requires the constant updating of programmes, anchored to the needs of the community and excellence in research. Multidisciplinarity, the completion of placements in the QI and the establishment of networks and centres of excellence are supported and encouraged. The QI seeks to be an ecosystem based on knowledge.

The industrial component: the QI has the largest concentration of IT workers in Canada. Its role is to showcase these businesses, but also those of other sectors, to improve collaboration between them and the various stakeholders and to promote the emergence of new ideas, while accelerating the innovation process. QI Montreal is a virtual and physical business ecosystem imbued with an entrepreneurial spirit.

> **Box 16. Montreal Quartier de l'Innovation** *(cont.)*
>
> Finally, the QI also has a social and cultural component. The strong presence of designers and innovators within the QI ensures that it is socially and functionally mixed, while promoting exchanges between arts, culture, technology and innovation. It is important to preserve this mixed nature and to make available to the various organisations in the district the various platforms and expertise of academic institutions, including that of the ETS engineering faculty and McGill University, two higher learning institutions particularly involved with the QI.

> **Box 17. "*Je vois/Je fais Montréal*"**
>
> On 17 November 2014, at the initiative of the Board of Trade of Metropolitan Montreal, the "*Je vois Montréal*" event was attended by over 1 500 people committed to Montreal's economic recovery. At the end of the event, participants committed to completing 181 projects structured around priority areas: attracting and retaining talent, business resilience and revitalising the living environment.
>
> "*Je vois Montréal*" bore witness to a reinvigoration of the lifeblood of the metropolis. The event confirmed citizens' deep attachment to their city. A follow-up project, "*Je fais Montréal*", was launched by the municipality of Montreal to support 181 projects in various stages of completion and to help create links and overcome barriers, including those of an administrative nature. Montrealers can follow, step-by-step, the progress of these projects on the "*Je fais Montréal*" website and can add their contribution.
>
> The "*Je fais Montréal*" project is also working on an index combining different dimensions of economic development and which takes into account investment, satisfaction among the users and beneficiaries of the programmes, the quality of the network of actors and social innovation. This indicator could be used not only to evaluate projects but also to assist policy makers alongside other economic development indicators.

In December 2015, the municipality also announced its support for the proposed creation of a private business school (see Box 18), the first of its kind in Montreal, with a financial contribution of CAD 632 000.

> **Box 18. The creation of the Montreal school of entrepreneurship**
>
> In September 2016, the Montreal's first private business school will be unveiled. This new training institution will offer training dedicated to all individuals wishing to develop their entrepreneurial skills. It differs from other training centres through its stated intention to lower barriers to entry, among other things. Prospective students will not have to be first enrolled at an educational institution, and enrolment fees are minimal, affordable and eligible for the school loan system.
>
> Promoted by the SAJE, a highly experienced organisation supporting young entrepreneurs, this initiative benefits from financial support from the Government of Quebec and the municipality of Montreal. It thus adds to the array of services offered to entrepreneurs by PME MTL. In addition to its premises located in the city centre, the school will open two satellite offices in the west and east of the Island of Montreal. It is therefore set to expand gradually in order to accommodate 1 550 entrepreneurs in 2018-19.

Montreal clusters

Montreal's nine industrial clusters, also called "metropolitan clusters", bring together key players, businesses and institutions playing a leading role in the development of an industry or grouping of connected activities (clusters). The value of developing industrial clusters includes a high degree of interaction between businesses and other associated players, allowing them collectively to grasp the changing economic circumstances, and to adapt to and benefit from them. The interaction between those involved in the clusters fosters innovation and economic learning. It is expected that businesses that form part of a cluster are more effective with regard to the supply of inputs, access to information, technology and institutions, and co-ordination of businesses in their sector.

The clusters each have their own specific features, including an industrial organisation with varying degrees of integration, sometimes dominated by a few large companies, such as in aerospace, or otherwise characterised by large numbers of SMEs, such as in information and communication technology (ICT) or even present in high value-added (life sciences) or more traditional (fashion) industries. But they also share common components or areas of work covering aspects such as the regulatory and fiscal framework, financing, innovation and marketing, promotion and influence, and the development and attraction of skills and talent. The research and innovation component takes shape in *ad hoc* initiatives, collaborations and institutions, but also in high-profile events.

The secretariats of the clusters, supported by industry stakeholders, the municipality of Montreal and the MMC, and the Governments of Quebec and Canada, play active roles, using various resources and tools, including rallying events that aim to develop a common strategic vision for partners. For example, the aerospace cluster regularly holds a forum on aerospace innovation.

In contrast to finance and aerospace, some clusters consist mainly of small businesses, which are more numerous, but whose resources are more limited. They therefore have less capacity for dialogue, even though their needs are greater, at least in regard to certain issues.

Many issues and challenges can be more specific, depending on the clusters, such as the transformation of the business model (life sciences), needs relating to emergence (new businesses in green technologies), modernisation (fashion), promotion (film and television), growth and marketing (ICT), diversification (aluminium) and public infrastructure (transport).

The clusters differ as to their relative weight in the Montreal economy and their potential for growth, innovation, and wealth and job creation. If no independent quantitative economic analysis seems to have addressed these aspects in the Montreal case, some studies conducted in the United States, for example, indicate that the existence of clusters does not in itself constitute a success factor for the businesses that form part of them (Morgan, 2007). According to these studies, the conditions that must be present for organisation into industrial clusters to deliver the expected results include the presence of a highly educated population.

Although the clusters can play a significant role in Montreal in terms of economic development, innovation and entrepreneurship, it is important to remember that the development of transverse technologies and contamination between business areas is crucial for the emergence of innovation processes. While links between participants in the different clusters are encouraged, whereby the second phase of development of the clusters includes an effort to organise collaboration between clusters (also called "inter-cluster"), it appears that collaboration so far remains limited, and that the clusters mainly operate in silos. The field of ICT is one that seems to lend itself more to collaborative experiences with other sectors, such as finance. The ICT cluster is also in discussions with the life sciences cluster on some issues, including that concerning personalised medicine made conceivable by big data, as well as with the aerospace cluster, given the key role played by ICT in this sector. Collaboration ideas are also under consideration in the project to develop a "green" aeroplane, where the aerospace cluster relies on collaboration with the green technology clusters.

Collaborations between the clusters and *Montréal International* (MI) also remain limited. However, by virtue of their respective duties, complementarities between clusters and MI should be supported in order to identify the needs and availability of skilled labour, and also to attract foreign investment in industries where Montreal has comparative advantages and a clear growth potential.

Universities and colleges: teaching, knowledge, research, technology transfer and collaboration with innovators

Given the link between the level of training of the workforce and key indicators, such as the level of productivity and income of the population, Montreal's higher education institutions play a key role in economic development, innovation and entrepreneurship, for example by fulfilling their primary mission of training people. Statistics Canada data obtained from the survey on the working population, and covering the careers of university and college graduates, demonstrate the high returns from advanced studies, irrespective of the field of study (Finnie et al., 2015).

Montreal's universities have made major efforts in recent years to reach out to the society in which they operate, including economic activity, in a number of ways. These efforts focus on enhancing internal research, supporting the recognition of intellectual property and the acquisition of patents, research partnerships with governments and the private sector, presence in several clusters, participation in projects such as the *Quartier de l'Innovation* and the establishment of incubators for their students. Universities also offer entrepreneurship and management courses in their various departments and faculties, which allows engineering, computing and social science students, and students from other disciplines to acquire basic knowledge in management, enabling them to go into business with the best chances of success in their endeavours.

Montreal's universities and their affiliated schools, including the *HEC Montréal* business school, the *Polytechnique Montréal* engineering school and the Dobson Center for Entrepreneurship at McGill University, have established departments and services designed to establish closer links with businesses and to stimulate entrepreneurship in their students and teaching staff.

Although they are in competition with each other to attract students and teachers, and to secure funding, Montreal's universities have increased the co-operation projects between them in recent years. For example, the ETS has partnered with McGill University in the *Quartier de l'Innovation* (QI) project, in which the knowledge economy component (training and research) is key. Concordia University has also joined this initiative as a major partner. Social innovation, anchored in improving citizens' quality of life, has also led to collaborations between the Montreal, McGill and UQAM universities, for example by contributing to the renovation of certain areas to make them more accessible to people with

> **Box 19. District 3 Innovation Center at Concordia University**
>
> Located within Concordia University, District 3 is an entrepreneurial community in the heart of downtown Montreal. Launched in 2013, this business incubator brings together people who collaborate, create and innovate. District 3 offers guidance, access to cutting-edge technology and opportunities for learning by doing. District 3 relies on donors, volunteers and mentors, coaches and students of entrepreneurship.
>
> The majority of start-up founders attending District 3 are recent university graduates who have the time, experience and financial support needed to launch a new business. District 3 enables Concordia to increase its influence within the community, with a customer base consisting of Concordia University graduates and graduates of other universities in Montreal.
>
> District 3 volunteers are primarily students, faculty members, staff members and graduates. A major private donation is used to finance three key initiatives: seed money, designed to help District 3 entrepreneurs classed as "makers" to focus on the design of prototypes; expanding the "Makerspace" open laboratory, secured by investments to equip District 3 with product development tools: sensors, laser cutters, 3D printers, etc.; and strengthening activities by hiring new District 3 staff as expert consultants or coaches.

reduced mobility or with major physical disabilities. Functioning as a network is becoming increasingly popular and fruitful, for example by enabling the pooling of resources and means. It is also necessary in a context of significant cuts in public financing.

Montreal's universities are faced with two main problems: difficulties relating to financing and the lack of recognition of higher education's contribution to the area's socio-economic development. French-speaking Quebec and Montreal residents received less schooling than their English-speaking counterparts for several decades, which has had the effect of limiting the appeal of university courses for a large part of the population. Montreal philanthropy is also less mature than in the rest of Canada, which has disadvantaged Quebec and Montreal-based universities. In general, they remain less well funded than their Canadian counterparts. Moreover, in the current context, Montreal-based universities need credible standard bearers that are convincing and capable of changing the understanding of the population in general, and of the higher political authorities in particular, as to their contribution to the prosperity of the Montreal metropolitan area. This is particularly evident in the case of foreign students choosing to study at one of Montreal's universities. Public policy objectives in higher education often focus on retaining graduates of Montreal's institutions after their studies. However desirable this goal of improving retention rates, it is also important to take a broader view of the contribution of higher education to the local economy. Foreign students who choose a Montreal-based university generate important spin-off effects by the mere fact of their living expenses, irrespective of their subsequent decisions. Moreover, even if these students decide to leave the metropolis after their studies, their contribution to the influence and prosperity of Montreal may nevertheless be significant. The contacts they maintain with their former classmates or their former teachers in Montreal allows them to operate with them as a network on projects, or even put them in touch with other people who may be likely to do business with Montreal-based businesses, to invest in them or set one up. In a globalised world, these contacts and networks can also be an asset for the Montreal economy. The more numerous and diverse they are, the more likely they are to contribute to the local community and its economy. This dimension is rarely taken into account when evaluating the beneficial effects of universities.

Collaboration between universities and colleges is almost non-existent in Montreal. The situation is paradoxical in many ways. First, an important duty of colleges is to prepare a majority of their students for university studies. It would therefore be desirable to share information about the prerequisites for university studies and to encourage a certain continuity of education between higher education levels. Second, colleges and universities employee a large number of teaching staff who are often recognised specialists in their respective fields, and these institutions have facilities and research contacts which could be pooled in connection with certain projects, for the benefit of all concerned. At present, competition prevails over co-operation between these teaching levels.

The involvement of Montreal's universities and colleges in initiatives such as the *Quartier de l'Innovation* demonstrate, however, that these institutions are continuing their efforts to reach out to economic players. In addition, organisations such as the College Centres for Technology Transfer (CCTTs, see Box 20), affiliated with CEGEPs and Quebec colleges, allow liaison between the activities of public training institutions and research in the private sector. Many SMEs, particularly micro-enterprises, refer to the CCTTs for their innovation needs, since the solutions proposed are less expensive than those of equivalent university centres. Private organisations such as NEOMED (see Box 21) also provide a link between basic research and those involved in the market entry of new products.

Box 20. **College Centres for Technology Transfer**

Ten College Centres for Technology Transfer (CCTTs) are located on the Island of Montreal, and several others in the rest of the metropolitan area. These institutions are the applied research centres of the CEGEPs and colleges of Quebec.

The CCTTs aim to assist businesses and organisations in innovation. This includes technical support, offering guidance in a process of technological change, adaptation of technological solutions or the transfer of knowledge and know-how; technological development, including the design, creation and improvement of products, the development and testing of processes or specialist equipment, the development or improvement of technologies, or even technology transfer; and information and training, through the development of customised training, technology monitoring, information retrieval, post-training follow up and evaluation, market research and feasibility studies, and by holding lectures and seminars.

The CCTTs of Montreal and surrounding areas bring together several hundred experts: researchers, engineers, technologists and specialists with PhDs, Master's or Bachelor's degrees or technical qualifications.

Box 21. **The NEOMED Institute**

The NEOMED Institute is a response to the changing R&D business model in the pharmaceutical industry. It seeks to bridge the gap between basic research and the market entry of new drugs.

The Institute provides industry expertise in drug discovery and development, combined with funding and a favourable environment for transforming innovations into therapeutic solutions. NEOMED drives drug discovery activities up to the stage of human proof of concept.

> Box 21. **The NEOMED Institute** *(cont.)*
>
> This stage is an important turning point, where projects become attractive to the biopharmaceutical industry or can constitute the basis for the creation of solid start-up companies.
>
> The Institute has two fully integrated research and development facilities: one in *Technoparc Montréal*'s Saint-Laurent Campus and the other in Laval. Both facilities function as open-access drug discovery hubs housing independent commercial businesses and providing a dynamic environment that fosters collaboration, innovation and creativity.
>
> The NEOMED Institute is jointly funded by the pharmaceutical industry, the Ministry of the Economy, Science and Innovation of Quebec, and the Networks of Centres of Excellence (NCE) of Canada.

Theme 4. Ensuring that growth is inclusive – economic development and skills development to promote the integration of all individuals into the labour market

Social inclusion is a major concern against a backdrop of relatively high unemployment – sometimes persistent in certain groups – and of growing inequality, with implications for longer-term growth prospects, cohesion and social justice. The role of education, training and labour market policies is widely recognised as critical in the long-term fight against exclusion and rising inequalities. Montreal's initiatives in response to these concerns target certain groups, including poorly educated young people, people with disabilities and immigrants.

Figure 3.5. **Inclusive growth**

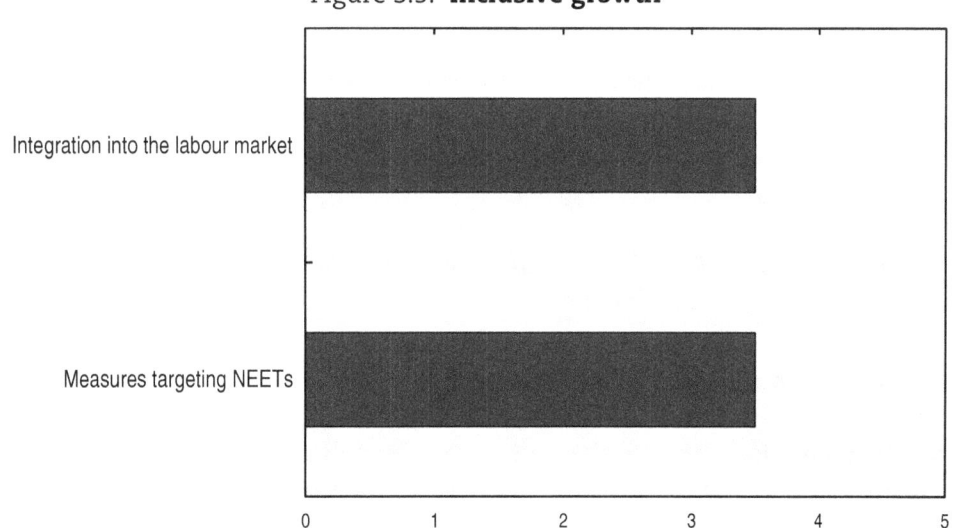

4.1. Adapting programmes to the needs of disadvantaged groups to facilitate their integration into the labour market

In Montreal, measures target and serve a wide range of groups, and some of these measures are aimed exclusively at them. Specific initiatives are undertaken to create jobs or to offer placement in jobs intended for people who are not ready to take up regular employment. These initiatives – such as subsidised employment opportunities or agreements with employers – often target beneficiaries of welfare assistance, whose characteristics (low level of schooling, prolonged absence from the labour market, drug addiction, etc.) prevent them from holding down productive and well-paying jobs in the short term. People with disabilities who, in many cases, should enjoy very long-term assistance with employment are a group specifically targeted by these measures. Adapted work centres (AWC), supported by *Emploi-Québec* and the Ministry of Health and Social Services, are an example of a programme enabling people whose employability potential is low to integrate into the labour market. These centres, four of which are operating in Montreal, offer a supervised work environment adapted to specific customers, and aim to improve the quality of life of their staff by promoting sound management practices.

Informal or illegal employment is not widespread in Montreal, at least based on the information available. Therefore, this issue is not considered a priority by public authorities, meaning support for people who wish to leave such jobs is at best *ad hoc*.

Specific programmes intended for immigrant populations

With a population of over 320 000 new immigrants who have been settled in Greater Montreal for less than 10 years, the area has seen one of North America's highest immigration levels (Montreal Metropolitan Community, 2013). In 2012, over 85% of immigrants who arrived in Quebec were headed for the Montreal metropolitan area. As discussed in Chapter 2 of this report, new immigrants to Montreal are primarily economic migrants, and the average education level among this population is much higher than that of non-immigrants.

Despite this, integration of immigrant populations into the labour market remains problematic. In 2014, the unemployment rate among immigrants who arrived less than 5 years ago was 18.5%, compared with 8.2% among the non-immigrant population. This rate was much higher than that observed in Toronto or in Vancouver and the average across Canada. In addition, as was shown in the second chapter of this report, the difficulties encountered by immigrants in the labour market persist over time. Furthermore, data on the degree of over-qualification of employees available at Quebec level (MICC, 2013) show that 43% of immigrants aged 25 to 54 in employment were overqualified in 2012, while this rate was 29.7% for workers as a whole. Immigrants who come to find a job therefore run a higher risk than the rest of the population of experiencing a mismatch between their qualification level and the skills required by their job.

Enabling immigrants to integrate into the local labour market effectively is nevertheless crucial in the Montreal demographic context, which features a progressively ageing population. In addition to maintaining a working age population of sufficient size, international immigration can also bring major benefits to the Montreal economy, particularly in terms of increasing the skills level of the workforce and innovation (Zhu, 2014). By stimulating local demand, creativity and knowledge spill-over effects, immigrants from diverse social and cultural backgrounds tend to encourage new investment and innovation processes.

Numerous organisations have implemented measures to promote the reception and integration of new immigrants in Montreal. For example, in the recognition of qualifications, *Qualification Montréal*, a unique inter-sectoral service, was set up in December 2013, at the initiative of *Éducation Montréal* and in collaboration with various education, training and labour market stakeholders. The Metropolitan Employment Council (CEM) has produced an action plan on the occupational integration of immigrants for the 2013-15 period and provides practical advice to employers to support them in their recruitment processes and migrant worker job retention efforts. Specific aids are also proposed, such as transportation, childcare, additional language or training courses to enable qualified immigrants to meet the specific requirements of Quebec professionals. Assessments are also conducted to measure progress recorded in combating the exclusion of these groups. Box 22 describes in more detail these three programmes set up by different institutions in order to achieve the goal of improved integration of immigrants into the labour market.

> **Box 22. Programmes for integrating immigrant populations into the labour market**
>
> **The Employment Integration Programme for Immigrants and Visible Minorities (PRIIME)**
>
> This programme, managed by *Emploi-Québec* and run in collaboration with MICC and *Investissement Québec*, aims to facilitate the employment of immigrant workers and workers from visible minorities. It consists of a series of incentive measures enabling, under certain conditions, the new employer of a targeted person to receive a wage supplement as well as a subsidy for associated supplementary costs, for example, for training or running specific integration activities during a given period.
>
> **The Nexus Employment programme**
>
> This programme of the municipality of Montreal offers businesses information, tools, support and resources for the recruitment and continued employment of foreign-trained professionals. The aim of the programme is to reduce the three main barriers to recruiting trained professionals from migrant backgrounds, namely actual or perceived difficulties in assessing qualifications, skills and international experience; lack of awareness of existing programmes to support employers in adapting their employees; and work environments ill-prepared for accommodating workers from migrant backgrounds. Montreal-based businesses from innovative sectors are eligible for the programme, and SMEs from these sectors are specifically targeted.
>
> **The Interconnection programme**
>
> The Interconnection programme, which the Board of Trade of Metropolitan Montréal (BTMM) runs in partnership with *Emploi-Québec*, aims to facilitate close contact between Montreal-based organisations and qualified new arrivals with a view to fostering their integration into the workforce. This programme aims to meet the needs of businesses and those of immigrants through an end-to-end, flexible scheme that includes free and varied twinning activities. Online registration is available to both immigrants and employers.

The impact of these various measures has long been limited as a result of a lack of co-ordination between the different organisations. To overcome this, in January 2016, the municipality of Montreal set up a single body, the Montreal Newcomers' Integration Office (BINAM), to bring together all services and funds allocated for the reception and integration of new immigrants. This new body was created especially to promote the practical implementation, at metropolitan Montreal level, of the federal government's commitment to accepting several tens of thousands of Syrian refugees in 2015 and 2016. Receiving USD 945 000 in funding for the year 2016, and with a dozen employees, BINAM enables the municipality of Montreal to develop internal expertise in the reception of immigrants, which it did not have previously. The municipality's objective is to offer an integration pathway through extended guidance focused on immigrants. This requires enough flexibility to tailor interventions to the profiles of the individuals and to the specific characteristics of the area, from a social, economic and cultural perspective.

Creating links with the world of work, for example by involving local employers, also appears to be crucial to ensuring that immigrants can have access to sustainable jobs and that the local economy fully benefits from this source of talent. Initiatives have emerged in various parts of the world to play an intermediary role between immigrants and employers, promoting mutual understanding of what they can each bring to each other and implementing practical links enabling immigrants to enter the job market. Closer to Montreal, the Toronto Region Immigrant Employment Council (see Box 23) offers an example of a facility that encourages the engagement of economic players regarding access to jobs for immigrant populations.

> **Box 23. Toronto Region Immigrant Employment Council (TRIEC)**
>
> The Toronto Region Immigrant Employment Council (TRIEC) brings together NGOs, businesses, unions and public policy officials in order to promote the employment of international migrants and to leverage the skills they bring to the city of Toronto. Local employers play a key role in TRIEC, whose chair is also chair of the Royal Bank of Canada. TRIEC also receives public-sector funding and support from a private foundation, the Maytree Foundation. This partnership has led to sponsorship programmes and large-scale internship programmes: in 2015, 1 338 skilled immigrants benefited from sponsorship by local employers.

4.2. Measuring the barriers to employment faced by certain groups and supporting initiatives aimed at addressing these barriers

The challenge of integrating young people who are not in education, employment or training (NEETs) into the labour market is considered a priority against the background of growing scarcity of people of working age and the need to raise average labour productivity levels.

As was explained in Chapter 2, the graduation rate in Montreal was 76% in 2014, although this rate is 78% across Quebec and 84% in Toronto (Toronto District School Board, 2014). Although the proportion of individuals leaving school without any qualifications has declined in Greater Montreal in recent years, its school dropout rates are high, especially in certain districts of the Island of Montreal. However, outlooks for labour market participation, unemployment and remuneration are all significantly lower for people who leave school without any qualifications, and this applies throughout their lives.

Montreal's economic players already undertake numerous initiatives to support disadvantaged young people and NEETs. For example, Montreal has an extensive network of youth employment centres (Centres Jeunesse Emploi) for this demographic group (see Box 24). Similarly, when a young person applies for social welfare, *Emploi-Québec* works with them and their service partners in order to guide them as quickly as possible towards initiatives that will lead them towards paid employment and economic and financial autonomy as soon as possible and under the best possible conditions.

Given our findings, particularly in certain districts, there is evidently still a long way to go before a clear majority of young people – particularly young men – are able to contribute

> **Box 24. Initiatives for young people: Carrefours jeunesse-emploi and Fusion Jeunesse**
>
> **Carrefours jeunesse-emploi (youth employment hubs)**
>
> *Carrefours jeunesse-emploi* are dedicated to providing education, employment and entrepreneurial support for young people, as well as personal and social support. There are 21 of these hubs on the Island of Montreal.
>
> *The Carrefour Jeunesse-Emploi Montréal Centre-Ville* works closely with the business community and local community. It helps young people aged 16 to 35, located temporarily or permanently in downtown Montreal, motivating them and supporting them in their educational, professional, creative and entrepreneurial endeavours with a view to finding a decent job in Montreal and elsewhere.
>
> **Fusion Jeunesse**
>
> *Fusion Jeunesse* is a charity. Its mission is to lower school dropout rates and create lasting links between the school system, the business community and community organisations working with young people, while implementing innovative and experiential education projects aimed at high-risk young people in order to contribute to their education, socialisation and qualification. This organisation has two offices in Montreal, and the head office of the organisation receives government support, as well as support from leading figures from the Montreal business community.
>
> *Fusion Jeunesse* is behind an innovative idea which had not yet been tested in Quebec or Canada: recruiting university students and sending them, as co-ordinators, into secondary schools in order to develop and support projects that motivate young people to excel creatively, encouraging them to become more involved in their academic success and stimulating their sense of belonging at school.

to Montreal's economy, which is increasingly focused on the knowledge and innovation industries, and to benefit fully in return. Combating school dropout rates therefore poses a major challenge and necessary condition for improving Montreal's socio-economic situation.

Note

1. For example, the Adult Education and Training Survey (AETS) covering the year 2002, and the Access and Support to Education and Training Survey (ASETS) covering data from 2008, both carried out by Statistics Canada.

References

BTMM (2016) *It's a Changing World: Let's Get Ready for the Jobs of the Future!*, Board of Trade of Metropolitan Montreal, www.emploisdufutur.com/en.html.

BDC (June 2010), *Canadian Entrepreneurship Status 2010*, Business Development Bank of Canada.

Cohendet, P. and B. Mazouz (2009), "Creative cities: Comparing Barcelona and Montreal", *Management International*, Vol. 13, Special Edition.

Cooke, P. (2001), "Regional Innovation Systems, Clusters, and the Knowledge Economy", *Industrial and Corporate Change*, Vol. 10, No. 4, pp. 945-974.

Finnie, R. et al. (2015), "Post-Schooling Outcomes of University Graduates: A Tax Data Linkage Approach", *Education Policy Research Initiative*, Working Paper No. 2015-01, Ottawa.

Froy, F. and S. Giguère (eds.) (2009), *Flexible Policy for More and Better Jobs*, Local Economic and Employment Development (LEED), OECD Publishing, Paris, http://dx.doi.org/10.1787/9789264059528-en.

Knudsen, B. et al. (2008), "Density and Creativity in US Regions", *Annals of the Association of American Geographers*, Vol. 98, pp. 461-478.

MICC (2013), *Éléments explicatifs de la surqualification chez les personnes immigrantes au Québec en 2012* [Explanations for over-qualification among immigrants to Quebec in 2012], 29 pages, Ministry of Immigration and Cultural Communities.

Montreal Metropolitan Community (décembre 2013), "Perspective Grand Montréal", *Bulletin de la Communauté métropolitaine de Montréal* n° 24, Montreal Metropolitan Community

Morgan, Q.J. (2007), *Industry Clusters and Metropolitan Economic Growth and Equality*, School of Government, University of North Carolina at Chapel Hill.

Mowat Centre (June 2013), *Making It Work: Final Recommendations of the Mowat Centre Employment Insurance Task Force, November 2011*, Mowat Centre, The Training Wheels Are Off.

Nelson, R. (2000), National Innovation Systems, in Z. J. Acs (ed.), *Regional Innovation, Knowledge and Global Change*, Routledge.

Niosi, J. and M. Zhegu (2011), *Study on Assistance with the Internationalization of Small and Medium-Size Quebec Enterprises*, Research Report funded by the Economic Development Agency of Canada.

OECD (2015a), *Job Creation and Local Economic Development*, OECD Publishing, Paris, http://dx.doi.org/10.1787/9789264215009-en.

OECD (2015b), *Employment and Skills Strategies in Flanders, Belgium*, OECD Reviews on Local Job Creation, OECD Publishing, Paris, http://dx.doi.org/10.1787/9789264228740-en.

OECD (2015c), *Back to Work: Canada: Improving the Re-employment Prospects of Displaced Workers*, OECD Publishing, Paris, http://dx.doi.org/10.1787/9789264233454-en.

OECD (2014a), *Employment and Skills Strategies in Canada*, OECD Publishing, Paris, http://dx.doi.org/10.1787/9789264209374-en.

OECD (2014a), *OECD Economic Surveys: Canada 2014*, OECD Publishing, Paris, http://dx.doi.org/10.1787/eco_surveys-can-2014-en.

OECD (2014b), *Employment and Skills Strategies in the United States*, OECD Reviews on Local Job Creation, OECD Publishing, Paris, http://dx.doi.org/10.1787/9789264209398-en.

OECD (2014c), "National programmes for SMEs and entrepreneurship in Italy", in OECD, *Italy: Key Issues and Policies*, OECD Publishing, Paris, http://dx.doi.org/10.1787/9789264213951-9-en

Puga, D. (2010), "The Magnitude and Causes of Agglomeration Economies", *Journal of Regional Science*, Vol. 50, No. 1, pp. 203-219.

Toronto District School Board (2014), *Graduation Rates*, www.tdsb.on.ca/HighSchool/GraduationRate.aspx.

Ville de Montréal (21 January 2016) *L'entrepreneuriat à Montréal: Un changement de culture s'opère à la Ville de Montréal, communiqué* [Entrepreneurship in Montreal: A change of culture in the municipality of Montreal, press release].

Zhu, N. (2014), *Synthèse de la littérature sur l'impact de l'immigration sur l'innovation* [Literature review on the impact of immigration on innovation], Ministry of Immigration, Diversity and Inclusion.

Chapter 4

An action plan for Montreal

> *An ambitious strategy taking simultaneous, co-ordinated action in a number of policy areas could help to strenghten the capacity of the Montreal economy to innovate and create high-quality jobs. This strategy will leverage Montreal's core asset – talent – and will seek to develop it further and build on it. The action should be led by an array of stakeholders acting in a new partnership framework. This chapter proposes an action plan for Montreal and its partners based on the analysis presented in this report.*

This report has identified the main strengths and weaknesses of the Montreal economy, focusing particular attention on the factors that play a direct role in job creation. The strong assets that Montreal possesses could allow it to become a major hub for inclusive growth and innovation in Canada, North America and beyond. These include a sound innovation ecosystem embracing a variety of stakeholders such as large industrial firms, start-ups in emergent sectors and top-flight universities; a plentiful and relatively well-trained workforce, although the proportion of highly skilled individuals could be higher; and a mature financial system. Furthermore, Quebec's largest city offers excellent working and living conditions, as well as a wealth of amenities that encourage innovative activities.

However, the city faces a number of challenges, including low productivity of workers, the lacklustre performance of a considerable share of the SME sector and the difficulties in finding work encountered by a significant section of the population, especially among immigrants. The analysis of the match between productive capacities and workforce skills shows that Montreal finds itself in a low skills equilibrium in comparison with other comparable North American metropolises, due to a deficit in both the supply of, and the demand for skills.

Finally, this report has cast light on the inadequacies of public policies and local initiatives for economic development, innovation, education and the labour market. There are many services to help businesses, but their resources are limited, and they are poorly co-ordinated. The many mechanisms to support local development do not take sufficient account of new approaches to economic development and innovation – these rely heavily on networks and partnerships between stakeholders in various sectors that are conducive to the pooling of resources and the transmission of knowledge. Employment agencies have room for manoeuvre that enables them to adjust their services to the specific nature of Montreal's labour market, but the same is not true of technical and vocational training establishments, which are still reliant on a relatively rigid, closed system that is slow to respond to the needs of local economic stakeholders. Despite the fact that there are several consultative bodies in existence, co-ordination between local initiatives and policies on employment, skills and economic development is not as good as it could be, partly reflecting the complex nature of the governance framework. Universities and CEGEPs could play a larger part as an ideas laboratory that could fuel local innovation and help SMEs to plan the next stages in their development. More could be done to encourage immigrants to enter the labour market and help qualified individuals to use their skills to benefit the Montreal economy.

Improving Montreal's ability to create more and better jobs means making more effective use of skills. Efforts must be made to make Montreal businesses fully aware of the potential that their employees' skills have for innovation and productivity gains, and to establish measures that will allow that potential to be realised. A better match between employees' qualifications and the jobs that they do would help to improve job quality and act as a strong incentive for younger generations to invest in training and acquire a high level of skills. Finally, better use of talent is conducive to immigrant populations finding work because it acknowledges the true value of having a diverse labour force that is open to the world.

Huge potential for improvement is within the reach of the municipality and its partners. Montreal has all the assets and ingredients to take up the challenge. Its strong leadership can and must grasp the opportunity that gaining a new institutional status represents. All stakeholders in the process should do likewise; by way of illustration, consider the case of the City Deals in the United Kingdom – it is in everyone's interest for Montreal to play its full part as the driver of economic and social progress in Quebec and beyond.

Better harnessing of talent to create more and better jobs is a goal that cannot be met through a national policy on its own, an isolated local initiative or a mere transfer of power. Only by adopting a comprehensive, coherent strategy that is actively pursued by all partners can the goal be reached. In view of this, the municipality of Montreal could play a greater role by rolling out an ambitious programme to transform public action and committing the region's entire political and socio-economic resources to it.

Montreal should devise a strategy that aims to put the city on the road towards a high-skills, high-productivity equilibrium in co-operation with its governmental and economic partners. The strategy should take the form of a series of specific, co-ordinated actions in the areas of economic development; innovation; education and training; integration of target groups, especially immigrants; and governance.

The first strand in the strategy will be to accelerate the development of SMEs and enhance the resilience of micro-enterprises. It is necessary to stimulate the development of SMEs' capabilities as exporters and to increase their willingness to innovate and invest. More small businesses must be reached and involved in pooling their experience so that they can learn to improve how they operate and organise their work.

A second strand will aim to boost innovation, particularly in its new guises, within the Montreal economy, and to accelerate the development of new ideas that can create jobs. This will involve strengthening cross-cutting innovation mechanisms and providing better links across the various creative sectors, cutting across sectoral strategies and purely technological innovation. The processes must help to develop productive activities while improving the use of Montreal's pool of talent.

A third strand will focus on skills development by encouraging demand for and use of skills in the Montreal economy. In a low-skills, low-productivity equilibrium, businesses tend to create poorer quality jobs (and the labour market tends to become sharply polarised), giving young people very little incentive to acquire high-level skills. Developing skills solely by raising the level of public education risks falling short of the target for creating high-quality jobs in a labour market that does not already provide enough jobs for highly qualified people. It will therefore be necessary to encourage businesses' use of available skills, as this is one of the key factors in innovation and job creation in the knowledge economy.

The fourth strand will supplement these robust skills-development actions and will take the form of measures to raise qualification levels. As demand for skills rises, it would be useful at the same time to boost the acquisition of higher-level qualifications so that supply can develop at the same rate as demand. This will allow the Montreal economy to move more quickly towards a high-skills equilibrium while preventing shortages in specialist, high-level skills.

The fifth strand will focus on greater harnessing of the skills and talent that have entered the country through immigration. This will involve better identification of skills that need to be sourced abroad, and better integration of individuals into the local labour market, allowing them to acquire any new skills they need and to draw on them in innovation processes. Immigration is a powerful driver of innovation and job creation, and it would be a pity not to fully encourage it.

As far as governance is concerned, it is vital for the action taken in pursuit of these strategic objectives to be part of an integrated framework that rallies all Montreal stakeholders around a common project. There are significant implications for the roles of all stakeholders involved in implementing public policy and local initiatives in Montreal. It is important to note them as part of the discussions that will grant greater responsibilities and resources to the municipality.

The remainder of this chapter will set out specific actions for each of these strands. It will conclude by indicating some implications for governance and institutional arrangements.

Strand 1. Structure, reinforce and more effectively target support for SMEs

Several recent initiatives have been launched in Montreal to encourage the development of entrepreneurship and to harmonise business support services in order to facilitate access. The municipality is active in this field; note in particular the launch of PME MTL (a network of experts supporting entrepreneurs and businesses) and support for a new training institution dedicated to entrepreneurship, in combination with provincial and federal government programmes. A large number of stakeholders – non-profit organisations, foundations – supplement these actions in the form of incubators or financial support for entrepreneurs. These measures are a step in the right direction given the relatively low propensity for people to become entrepreneurs.

These actions should be developed further and strengthened, but more must be done to assist SMEs specifically in their development. The majority of SMEs do little to innovate and invest. They do not try to improve their work organisation or to identify new markets. Although a number of SMEs participate in activities organised within the framework of industrial clusters and work with their sectoral partners, this is often not enough to generate a shift towards strategies to move into higher value-added markets and more efficient production processes that make optimum use of employees' skills.

Promote SMEs internationalisation. The plethora of programmes and services directed at SMEs by the various tiers of government could, like those offered by PME MTL, be strengthened further and better aligned in order to enhance their effectiveness and reach the majority of SMEs and micro-enterprises. The processes of internationalisation and innovation often go hand in hand and are mutually reinforcing within businesses; it would therefore be desirable to allocate more funds to support the development of SMEs in new national and international markets, in close co-ordination with actions that promote innovation. Internationalisation as a goal could be developed in the form of business leader training, technical assistance, finance and mentoring, as part of programmes and services directed at SMEs in a way that encourages synergies. For example, business bridges could be developed like the one planned with the municipality of Lyon that will enable SMEs from both cities to have access to innovation support facilities in both Lyon and Montreal (including accelerators and incubators), so that even in the early stages of growth, there is encouragement to market products in Quebec, France and even Europe and North America.

Stimulate innovation within SMEs. For those businesses that will always focus on the local market given the nature of the product or service they provide, a process of innovation from the inside would appear necessary. Whether technological or not, innovation often arises from interactions between the staff of one business and the staff of its partners in the value chain, i.e. its customers or suppliers. Innovation can also arise from interactions within a business's local ecosystem, which includes businesses it works with, those it competes with, government services, consultants and external technical staff. New ideas for improvements, whether they relate to methods of production or the use of inputs, can emerge from new products and services, or from new business strategies that lead to new opportunities and potential career progression for staff. It is vital that this kind of innovation, which requires some degree of open-mindedness on the part of the business leader, is free to thrive within the business. It may take the form of technical assistance and management training for firms to encourage them to move towards higher-skilled methods of production and services. Arrangements that encourage occupational mobility within a company can also enhance productivity by increasing employee motivation. Finally, both leaders and employers should be encouraged to undertake further training throughout their careers in order to upgrade their managerial skills. Recent work to reorganise the support network for Montreal enterprises, resulting in the creation of PME MTL, is part of that approach and should be developed further in order to broaden awareness of practices that encourage innovation within organisations and the optimum use of skills within firms.

Strand 2. Encourage bottom-up and cross-cutting innovation processes

In view of the large number of stakeholders involved in supporting economic development in Montreal, the system of governance is relatively complex. The stakeholders' strategies do not dovetail perfectly even though significant effort has been made to ensure that they do. Further progress is required to streamline and co-ordinate public action, along with a change in approach to adjust it to the new local development and innovation environment.

The importance of network strategies in innovation processes has been noted in this report. Against a background of the emergent knowledge economy, agglomeration economies give dense urban areas a crucial advantage in terms of productivity and innovation by promoting the transmission of knowledge, the pooling of resources and the matching of supply and demand on the markets for goods, services and labour (Puga, 2010). Given its critical mass and significant resources, especially in terms of human capital, Montreal should be able to benefit from such agglomeration economies.

Moreover, the role of public authorities in fostering local development is also changing as "bottom-up" local development strategies are emerging. These strategies give socio-economic stakeholders greater freedom to seal partnerships in order to develop projects that draw on local resources. That approach should make it possible to adopt dovetailed, multisectoral local development strategies that are geared to local potential and needs, and that encourage involvement of a large number of stakeholders within networks.

Continue to support collaborative initiatives that mobilise all stakeholders. In that context, public authorities in Montreal can play a major role in rallying and networking the city's many innovation and economic development stakeholders. Greater co-ordination between these stakeholders would enable them to achieve better leverage for their investments in innovation, skills development and the identification of new markets. The initiative "Je vois Montréal" and its successor "Je fais Montréal" fully reflect this approach to rallying socio-economic stakeholders in order to produce a shared view of the current situation and the future of the region, and to encourage the formation of partnerships that will carry out real projects. There should be more action in this vein to ensure that it reaches a broader population of local stakeholders such as young entrepreneurs and organisations working in neighbourhoods that are currently sidestepped by economic initiatives and innovation streams.

Broaden innovation processes. The municipality should continue to act as a catalyst and facilitator while ensuring that stakeholder projects incorporate the goal of making more effective use of skills, for example by including innovations in staff management, employee training or occupational mobility. Traditional technological processes should continue to be encouraged, including through industrial clusters, but it would be desirable to step up support both for projects such as "living labs" that view individuals and users as key players in innovation processes, and for settings that encourage meetings, the exchange of practices and approaches, creativity and experimentation. This support must be ongoing, patient and respectful of the independence of the stakeholders concerned.

De-compartmentalise industrial clusters. The municipality and its partners should continue their active involvement in promoting industrial clusters and growing sectors. They should also continue with their work to de-compartmentalise clusters. The promotion of industrial clusters produces positive results in terms of innovation but can be counter-productive if it has the effect of restricting interaction and the exchange of ideas between sectors. Closed sectoral innovation systems can also embed processes within sectors and delay their development. Initiatives in other places, such as Flanders (see Box 9), show that it is important to supplement sectoral innovation systems with cross-cutting innovation systems that try to pool practices and encourage exchanges and co-operation across sectors.

Strand 3. Stimulate demand for skills through training and research

This report has demonstrated that Montreal has a supply- and demand-side skills deficit in relation to other comparable North American metropolises. In a low-skills, low-productivity equilibrium, businesses tend to create poorer quality jobs, making young people reluctant to acquire high-level skills. Employers' lacklustre training programmes, the relatively weak performance of Montreal SMEs and their apparent lack of international ambition are consistent with this report's finding that demand for skills among employers is weak. That is why improving productivity and job quality in Montreal must involve the adoption of a comprehensive, coherent strategy that aims to develop the skills of the labour force alongside the production capabilities of the local economy. All public, private and civil society stakeholders involved, first and foremost training and research organisations, should put co-ordinated measures in place to achieve that common goal.

In order to stimulate demand locally, it is important to embed skills-development policies in broader mechanisms for business support and strategic development (OECD, 2015a). As stated above, this can take the form of technical assistance and management training for firms to encourage them to move towards higher-skilled methods of production and services, or raise their product market strategies. The initiatives put in place by the municipality, such as PME MTL, can play an important role in encouraging better utilisation of skills in SMEs. The scale of the task however, goes far beyond the level that current capabilities can address, given that it involves improving the productivity of a large pool of small and micro-enterprises.

A number of stakeholders, particularly in the training sector, could also become involved and contribute to this difficult and important task because it is vital to reach a large number of SMEs, particularly micro-enterprises. Micro-enterprises usually have no human resources management service and do not have the capacity to introduce measures to promote staff training, mobility or the emergence of internal innovation processes. *Emploi-Québec* conducts some activities in that regard, but they would appear to fall short given the need to inject vitality into the vast SME sector in Montreal.

Strengthen links between educational institutions and firms, especially SMEs, to promote skills utilisation through applied research. Educational establishments, especially CEGEPs, can play an important role in developing businesses' capacities, especially those of small businesses, to use their workforces' skills in an innovative fashion. Despite their varying capabilities, some CEGEPs have already started to produce assessments and services for SMEs on human resources management, labour demand planning and the identification of skills gaps. They have drawn up training programmes tailored to the needs of business leaders and their employees, as well as technical assistance services. That role should be developed further and receive better funding. Some of the technical aspects should be conducted in partnership with other players such as PME MTL. The partnership with *Emploi-Québec* will also be vital, particularly given the fact that, as a public employment service, it can identify businesses that have a high turnover of staff, which can be symptomatic of poor work organisation, inadequate processes and low productivity.

Encourage universities to actively align with and engage in local economic development priorities. Universities often make a significant contribution to the economic prosperity of the regions where they are located, including by playing a role in providing training and attracting skills, as well as acting as incubators for new ideas that could be brought to market by the local economy. In Montreal, their contribution to local economic prosperity would appear to be less than their potential would suggest, partly reflecting difficulties in retaining talented students once they complete their studies, and partly because they do not appear to be strongly affected by the difficulties of the local economy. Montreal's universities are particularly well-placed in so far as international research goes. Additionally, they take part in technology transfer and work with businesses, generally large ones, to bring new products to market and refine more efficient production processes. Although they have set up centres for entrepreneurship and new business incubators, there is no question that their applied research activities aimed at smaller local businesses could be developed further. CEGEPs have an important role to play in this regard through the College Centres for Technology Transfer (CCTTs) that provide solutions that are often well-matched to the needs of Montreal SMEs and micro-enterprises. It would appear necessary to work with local businesses to encourage a closer link between the academic world and technical and vocational training in order to boost applied research and improve the dissemination of its outcomes among SMEs. Incremental innovation within firms of all sizes, for example by utilising technologies in production processes, could lead to productivity gains. Better employment opportunities within local industry could then benefit the talented people attracted to the university. The development of working relationships between the universities and the CEGEPs would pool these institutions' knowledge of the local economy and investment capacity, putting this knowledge at the service of local employers.

Facilitate employer engagement in the design of vocational education and training curricula. Employer participation in designing programmes encourages their use and increases responsiveness to the needs of businesses and industry, as is the case in Ontario and the

United States (see Box 5), for example. Programmes that are more relevant to market needs and that involve employers in their delivery are more attractive to young people and can lead to greater participation, result in better learning and foster innovation within businesses. As the management of technical and occupational training becomes more flexible, it could be supplemented by involving employers more readily in programme design and delivery.

Strand 4. Raise the level of skills of the workforce

A comprehensive strategy that aims both to develop productive capacities and achieve better use of skills should be able to increase incentives to acquire more skills. While this gradual approach is necessary, the relatively low level of qualifications currently held by the Montreal population should not be overlooked, as this acts as a drag on the city's social and economic development. Qualifications have an impact not only on economic growth, but also on employment and inclusion outcomes. Within the OECD, 80% of people with a university diploma are employed, but the figure is only 70% for those with a secondary education diploma. The differences in income between various categories of the population based on qualification levels are generally substantial (OECD, 2015b). While investing in skills supply alone would most likely lead to disappointing results if there is no matching effort on the demand side, putting in place an ambitious strategy to raise the level of skills among the Montreal population seems advisable.

Make technical and vocational training more flexible. Education and vocational training are relatively inflexible in Quebec because the system of training approvals is centralised, restricting the scope for courses to adapt to the needs of economic actors and individuals. The CEGEPs need greater flexibility to adjust the courses they offer to students who are at risk of dropping out and to dropouts who want to take up training. The lack of flexibility is also evident in training offered to adults; it often has strict entry criteria that restrict opportunities for individuals without secondary school qualifications who want to return to the classroom and develop their careers. The approvals system could be adjusted across the city by increasing local responsibilities. Greater flexibility, which would make it possible to tailor courses more closely to the specific features of the local economy and the social environment of the various neighbourhoods, could encourage various groups in society to acquire more qualifications.

Smooth educational pathways through partnerships between universities and community colleges (CEGEPS). A closer link between universities and CEGEPs could foster a rise in qualifications by encouraging young people who otherwise would not necessarily have done so to continue with their studies. Greater continuity in training pathways and better information on university courses and vocational opportunities could better prepare students in CEGEPs for higher education. Additionally, CEGEPs and universities could, in conjunction with their partners on the labour market, pool their knowledge of the Montreal economy and jointly identify the sectors and job profiles that could benefit from higher levels of qualifications along with ways to promote progress in that direction.

Strand 5. Facilitate the integration of immigrants into the labour market and leverage their potential for boosting innovation

The Montreal agglomeration currently receives close to 35 000 immigrants per year, or around 70% of all immigrants arriving in Quebec, and the municipality must be ready to welcome a significant share of the 25 000 Syrian refugees that the Federal Government undertook to re-settle in 2016. Like many other large urban areas in the OECD, Montreal must address the challenge posed by an ageing population, and international immigration could be a means of maintaining a sufficient pool of qualified labour to meet local employers' needs. Immigration can also be a major asset in terms of improving the supply of skills and providing the impetus for innovation processes.

The current situation for immigrants on the Montreal labour market is unsatisfactory both in terms of the level of unemployment and the mismatch between individuals' qualifications and the skills required for the jobs that they do. Given that there are many bodies in Montreal involved in supporting the integration of immigrants, the profile of their actions and their effectiveness have long been inadequate. The establishment of the Montreal Newcomers' Integration Office (BINAM) in January 2016 may help to put some of these matters right.

Ensure that Montreal's skills needs are taken into account when determining provincial intakes of skilled immigrants. Measures should be taken to improve the link between the skills supplied by immigrants and demand from employers. The municipality should help to draw up a list of potential unmet future skills needs and be involved in the decision-making process leading to the identification of immigration needs and their distribution across the Montreal region.

Better tailor training offers to the needs of immigrants. In view of the rapid changes in the labour market, training offered to immigrants should be more responsive to the needs of individuals and local firms. There must be better communication between bodies providing training and bodies concerned with business demand. Accordingly, employers could be encouraged to become involved in drawing up training programmes. The municipality should be able to bring training bodies and employers' representatives together to improve the co-ordination and planning of training programmes. As mentioned previously, it would be desirable for these training programmes to be made sufficiently flexible so that they can be tailored more precisely to immigrants' circumstances. They should also be responsive, adjustable and able to be scheduled at various times of the year, including for small groups.

Ensure that the process of streamlining support services for immigrants priorities labour market integration and attachment. Policy tools and instruments should be geared to immigrants' particular needs and include specialist support to encourage their acculturation and develop their social networks. It is also vital to provide employers with solutions to overcome barriers to the employment of immigrant job candidates, including through help to validate diplomas and work experience gained abroad, the acquisition of adequate language skills and the provision of vocational training. The establishment of the BINAM is part of a process to tailor measures to individuals' specific needs and provide better co-ordination across the various bodies in the field. Establishing lasting links between the BINAM and partners on the labour market would appear essential to helping immigrants find work while making more effective use of the reservoir of talent that immigrant populations represent for the local economy.

Facilitate enterprise creation by immigrants. Promoting entrepreneurship among immigrant populations can also contribute to their integration into Montreal society. The specific measures that can be taken in that field include offering advice on the local legal system or drawing up business plans. In these matters, it is vital to be able to empathise with immigrant groups' viewpoints so that integration can occur as quickly as possible and optimum use can be made of immigrants' entrepreneurial potential. Given that entrepreneurship in Montreal is relatively weak, the effect on the local economy could be particularly beneficial.

Put in place tailored support for youth of immigrant origin. Given the difficulties that some young immigrants are experiencing getting fully integrated within Montreal society, it may be necessary to take measures more specifically targeted to these individuals. Mentoring programmes could provide them with the opportunity to gain a greater appreciation of their qualities and their labour market potential; to improve their knowledge of the education system, training opportunities and the transition to the world of work; and, as a result, to raise their aspirations and ambitions. It is also important to support young people even after they have secured their first job so that they do not become stuck in poor quality jobs and are able to take their careers forward. Identifying and working in partnership with employers in key growth sectors can improve opportunities for sustainable employment for young people with poor skills.

Implications for governance and metropolitan status

In light of the analysis set out in this report, these are the courses of action required if no stone is to be left unturned in ensuring that Montreal can create more and better jobs in a more productive economy in the future. Only a combination of bold actions involving productive capacities, skills, the use of those skills, and the talent available in Montreal can put its economy on the path towards a high-skills, high-productivity equilibrium.

The actions required involve a diverse range of stakeholders. They cover the municipality of Montreal as well as the various tiers of government. Accordingly, the recommendations can feed into the current discussions between the municipality and the Government of Quebec on granting Montreal with a new institutional status.

A significant proportion of the recommendations relate to **the management** of a number of public policies that are the responsibility of the Government of Quebec. They include a recommendation for the government to be able to make certain aspects of education and technical and vocational training more flexible. Implementation of this recommendation is an important matter. It is unclear, and it was not the subject of this report, whether greater flexibility in these areas could be beneficial to all localities of Quebec. However, it is undeniable that Montreal occupies a unique economic and social position in Quebec, and that the full realisation of its potential would benefit the entire Quebec economy. Consequently, it may be desirable for the public authorities to consider affording the municipality the opportunity to participate in the co-determination of strategic objectives and the procedures for delivering public policy in these fields.

In particular, the following points would appear to be important: technical and vocational training courses should be subject to more rapid approval processes, and decisions should be taken at metropolitan level in order to meet metropolitan strategic objectives; partnerships should involve employers in the design and delivery of technical and vocational training; the entry criteria for adult training programmes should be more flexible, and the resources allocated to such programmes should be increased to make them a more powerful lever for integration and skills upgrading; immigration needs and the distribution of immigrants in line with skills profiles should be co-determined at metropolitan level; and training programmes for immigrants should be adjustable in terms of their content, their scheduling and their duration.

Other recommendations relate to **the strategic framework** for government policy. This is true of the role that CEGEPs could play in helping businesses to make better use of the available skills. This task could be beefed up, clarified and better resourced in the Montreal region. The services provided to young people following immigration should also be enhanced and better geared to the needs of target groups in the region.

The Quebec Government could **set up incentives** to guide actions from other stakeholders. Institutions in some fields identify their own targets and enjoy great leeway as to how they meet the targets they set themselves. This is true of higher education: universities set their own objectives and identify the local and international action required in order to achieve them, even though a significant portion of their funding comes from the provincial government's budget. The governmental authorities can play an important role in encouraging them to gear their actions to the strategic needs of the urban area and its socio-economic environment, supporting a proactive city-led approach towards its partners in the world of education. Public authorities have other resources, including funding, that they can use to incentivise such major stakeholders to adopt a more collaborative approach at the level of the city. Among other things, those resources will have to be used to encourage the universities and CEGEPs to work together to channel more people towards university education; and to strengthen the role of universities in the development of the Montreal economy.

Through its leadership, the municipality of Montreal will have a multi-faceted role in implementing the actions to be taken in the various fields outlined in this report.

First and foremost, it will involve **establishing, piloting or strengthening** certain mechanisms. For example, the services that the municipality provides to support SMEs should focus more on internal innovation and internationalisation. Acting closely with its partners, bold action should be taken, targeting many SMEs and especially micro-enterprises, to persuade them to improve the use of their employees' skills and encourage training and career progression. The municipality should also beef up the bottom-up initiatives in place to harness and generate innovation, such as "Je vois/je fais Montréal", and broaden them so that they can provide avenues for making more effective use of the skills available within Montreal's businesses.

Next, Montreal will have to embrace a new **federative role** for organisations to plug the gaps in the existing framework and, as necessary, strengthen actions in the areas where it does not have a central role. This will be necessary in order to de-compartmentalise industrial clusters where a number of stakeholders are involved. The municipality will have a key role in tailoring programmes and services for immigrants, including creating links between employers, training providers and immigrant groups, drawing on experiences elsewhere in Canada.

The municipality can leverage its strong leadership to **involve the private sector** and secure its support in its pursuit of the various objectives. Whether this involves internationalising SMEs and improving the use of skills, involving employers in designing training programmes, encouraging bottom-up innovation or building linkages between training and services to support the integration of immigrants, the partnership with the private sector will be key to a successful outcome. The Mayor should give Montreal businesses an important role in directing and implementing a number of key actions while remaining focused on this important objective.

Above all, Montreal can go further and provide a **strong example of integration**. Like Lyon and Manchester, which have been given enhanced powers in certain policy areas and have used them to take a broader approach to socio-economic development in their cities, Montreal can project a long-term comprehensive, motivational vision. The move towards a new status for the municipality of Montreal offers an opportunity to move towards greater integration of strategies for economic development, employment and skills development at metropolitan level. Although the municipality does not have competence in education and training, it should appreciate how crucial it is to have strong co-ordination at metropolitan level in this policy area. It is essential for the municipality to play a new role to increase the involvement of universities, CEGEPs and employers in the joint project and to encourage the synergies between them.

Finally, the municipality could play an important role **by vouching for** a successful outcome for the strategy. In order to succeed, the project must be based on an accountability principle. A broad array of stakeholders wants to help make Montreal a city of talent in North America. Through strong leadership, the Mayor is well placed to bring together people from the areas of business, research, education, training and social integration from the public, private and non-governmental sectors throughout the Montreal region. The Mayor also have the major advantage of being able to involve various tiers of metropolitan governance as needed. Like all partnership projects, however, bureaucratic delay and lack of commitment are to be anticipated. By assuming responsibility for the project and reflecting that responsibility in a requirement to be accountable for all partners involved, the Mayor could do more than anyone else to achieve the desired outcome and to make the change in status the trigger for Montreal's transformation.

References

OECD (2015a), *Job Creation and Local Economic Development*, OECD Publishing, Paris, http://dx.doi.org/10.1787/9789264215009-en.

OECD (2015b), *The Future of Productivity*, OECD Publishing, Paris, http://dx.doi.org/10.1787/9789264248533-en.

Puga, D. (2010), "The Magnitude and Causes of Agglomeration Economies", *Journal of Regional Science*, Vol. 50, No. 1, pp. 203-219.

ORGANISATION FOR ECONOMIC CO-OPERATION AND DEVELOPMENT

The OECD is a unique forum where governments work together to address the economic, social and environmental challenges of globalisation. The OECD is also at the forefront of efforts to understand and to help governments respond to new developments and concerns, such as corporate governance, the information economy and the challenges of an ageing population. The Organisation provides a setting where governments can compare policy experiences, seek answers to common problems, identify good practice and work to co-ordinate domestic and international policies.

The OECD member countries are: Australia, Austria, Belgium, Canada, Chile, the Czech Republic, Denmark, Estonia, Finland, France, Germany, Greece, Hungary, Iceland, Ireland, Israel, Italy, Japan, Korea, Latvia, Luxembourg, Mexico, the Netherlands, New Zealand, Norway, Poland, Portugal, the Slovak Republic, Slovenia, Spain, Sweden, Switzerland, Turkey, the United Kingdom and the United States. The European Union takes part in the work of the OECD.

OECD Publishing disseminates widely the results of the Organisation's statistics gathering and research on economic, social and environmental issues, as well as the conventions, guidelines and standards agreed by its members.

LOCAL ECONOMIC AND EMPLOYMENT DEVELOPMENT (LEED)

The OECD Programme on Local Economic and Employment Development (LEED) has advised governments and communities since 1982 on how to respond to economic change and tackle complex problems in a fast-changing world. Its mission is to contribute to the creation of more and better quality jobs through more effective policy implementation, innovative practices, stronger capacities and integrated strategies at the local level. LEED draws on a comparative analysis of experience from the five continents in fostering economic growth, employment and inclusion. For more information on the LEED Programme, please visit *www.oecd.org/cfe/leed*.